NEW ENGLISH ICEBREAK
잉글리시 아이스브레이크

Advanced

THE TPR GRAPHICS BOOK For students of all ages

by Prize-Winning instructor, Ramiro Garcia &
edited by James J. Asher, Ph. D,
originator of the Total Physical Response, known worldwide as TPR

Copyright © 2008 Sky Oaks Productions, Inc.
P.O. Box 1102
Los Gatos, CA 95031 USA
www.tpr-world.com
Phone: (408) 395 7600
Fax: (408) 395 8440
Korean translation copyright © Watermelon Company, 2012

This Korean edition was published by Watermelon Company in 2012
by arrangement with Sky Oaks Productions Inc.

이 책의 한국어판 저작권은 Sky Oaks Productions Inc. 와 독점 계약한
Watermelon Company 에 있습니다.
저작권법에 의하여 한국 내에서 보호를 받는 저작물이므로 무단전재와 복제를 금합니다.

NEW ENGLISH ICEBREAK
엉글리시 아이스브레이크
Advanced

Watermelon

Ramiro Garcia
20여 년 동안 고등학교와 성인 어학 교실에서 성공적으로 많은 학생들을 가르쳐 왔다.
특히 그의 학습 방법은 영어를 사용하지 않는 많은 나라에서 온 거의 반벙어리 상태의
영어 학습자들을 상대로 즉각적이고 유쾌한 효과를 거두고 있다.

Dr. James J. Asher
휴스턴대학과 뉴멕시코대학에서 텔레비전 저널리즘과 심리학으로 박사 학위를 받았다.
그 후, 워싱턴대학과 스탠포드대학에서 언어학, 교육심리학의 연구 생활을 계속하였다.
외국어 과목에서 성적이 매우 우수하였음에도 불구하고 말하는 데에 어려움을 겪은
그는 외국어 교습법에 관심을 갖고 연구를 하여 오른쪽 뇌를 이용한 기억 방식 이론을
창안하였다. 그의 교육 이론은 현재 전 세계 국가에 널리 활용되어 언어 교육의 가장
효과적인 교습법으로 검증되고 있다.

1판 1쇄 인쇄 2012년 9월 30일
1판 1쇄 발행 2012년 10월 10일

펴낸이	정중모
펴낸곳	Watermelon
등록	2003년 9월 3일(제300-2003-162호)
주소	서울시 마포구 잔다리로 2길 7-0
전화	02-3144-1304
팩스	02-3144-0775
홈페이지	www.yolimwon.com
이메일	toctalk@yolimwon.com
카페	http://cafe.naver.com/engicebreak

* 책값은 뒤 표지에 있습니다.
ISBN 978-89-7063-749-5 14740
　　　978-89-7063-747-1 (세트)

Preface

"비영어권 국가에서 온 반벙어리 외국인들에게 즉각적이고 유쾌한 효과를 거둔 영어 교재"

막연히 영어가 어렵다고 생각하는 분들을 위해 만들어진 이 책을 가만히 따라가기만 해도 어느새 영어에 친해져 있는 여러분의 모습을 발견하게 됩니다.

100% Graphic Language Book

이 책은 그림으로 표현된 영어책입니다.
그림이 주는 효과는 크게 두 가지로
보는 즉시 내용을 알게 함과 동시에
우뇌를 자극해 기억을 쉽게 할 수 있도록
도와줍니다.

망각 곡선에 근거한 자연스런 반복

이 책의 모든 그림과 스크립트는 불규칙적으로 여러 번 반복됩니다.
보통 7번 정도의 우연한 만남이 있어야 대상을 확실히 기억할 수 있다고 하는데 자연스런 반복을 통해 이 책은 영어의 기본을 정확히 여러분 몸에 심어 드릴 것입니다.

How to use this book

Don't Study!

공부하는 책이 아닙니다! 그냥 눈으로 훑어 보아도 되고 무료로 제공되는 MP3 파일을 들으면서 보면 효과는 더욱 커집니다. 뜻이 궁금하면 밑에 작게 적어 넣은 해석을 보면 됩니다.

Don't Repeat!

책장을 앞뒤로 넘길 필요가 없습니다. 잊을 만하면 자연스럽게 다시 반복되니 페이지 넘어가는 대로 그냥 넘기면서 페이지의 지시에 잘 따르기만 하면 됩니다.

Just Imagine & Listen!

그림은 내용을 바로 알게 해 주는 장점과 함께 상상력을 자극해 다른 표현과 상황을 덤으로 알려 줍니다.

Contents

CHAPTER 1
Graphic Sheets 1

- Lesson 1 — 10
- Lesson 2 — 30
- Lesson 3 — 50
- Lesson 4 — 70

CHAPTER 2
Graphic Sheets 2

- Lesson 5 — 96
- Lesson 6 — 116
- Lesson 7 — 136
- Lesson 8 — 156

CHAPTER 3
Dictation Sheets 1

- Lesson 1 — 182
- Lesson 2 — 202
- Lesson 3 — 222
- Lesson 4 — 242

CHAPTER 4
Dictation Sheets 2

- Lesson 5 — 268
- Lesson 6 — 288
- Lesson 7 — 308
- Lesson 8 — 328

ENGLISH
ICEBREAK

Chapter 1

Lesson 1 - 4   Graphic Sheets 1

Lesson 1

step 01
START ···▶

01

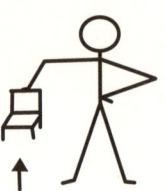

The man is lifting the chair.

02

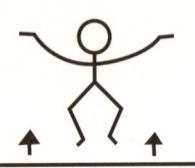

The guy is flying.

03

A person touches the chair.

04

A girl is writing her name on the blackboard.

05

The guy is putting a box on the table.

The man is lifting the chair. 남자가 의자를 들어 올리고 있다   The guy is flying. 남자가 날고 있다   A person touches the chair. 한 사람이 의자를 만진다   A girl is writing her name on the blackboard. 여자아이가 칠판에 이름을 쓰고 있다   The guy is putting a box on the table. 남자가 상자를 테이블 위에 놓고 있다

06

There is a hat.

07

Pen has a pointy end.

08

There are two houses.

09

There is space between the two tables.

10

Square has four sides.

Go on to the next step!

There is a hat. 모자가 있다   Pen has a pointy end. 펜은 끝이 뾰족하다   There are two houses. 집이 두 채 있다   There is space between the two tables. 두 테이블 사이에 공간이 있다   Square has four sides. 정사각형은 네 개의 변이 있다

step 02
START ···▶

01

The man is smelling something on the table.

02

A guy drops something into the box.

03

A guy is standing up.

04

A person is picking up something off the table.

05

A guy is kneeling.

The man is smelling something on the table. 한 남자가 테이블 위 뭔가의 냄새를 맡고 있다   A guy drops something into the box. 한 남자가 뭔가를 상자 안에 떨어뜨린다   A guy is standing up. 남자가 일어서고 있다   A person is picking up something off the table. 한 사람이 테이블에서 뭔가를 집어 들고 있다   A guy is kneeling. 한 남자가 무릎을 꿇고 있다

06

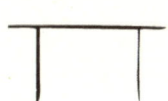

There is a table.

07

Apple is delicious.

08

The guy is supporting something over his head.

09

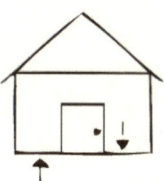

People come to the house in and out.

10

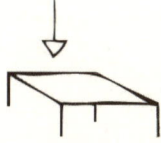

There is nothing behind the table.

● ● ● ▶

Go on to the next step!

There is a table. 테이블이 있다   Apple is delicious. 사과는 맛있다   The guy is supporting something over his head. 한 남자가 머리 위로 무언가를 받치고 있다   People come to the house in and out. 사람들이 집 안팎을 왔다 갔다 한다   There is nothing behind the table. 테이블 뒤에는 아무것도 없다

step 03
START ⋯▶

A person turns the light bulb on.

02

A person is hiding under the table.

03

A guy is pointing at the light bulb.

04

A boy is clapping.

05

The teacher is drawing a house on the blackboard.

A person turns the light bulb on. 한 사람이 전구를 켠다   A person is hiding under the table. 한 사람이 테이블 밑에 숨어 있다   A guy is pointing at the light bulb. 한 남자가 전구를 가리키고 있다   A boy is clapping. 남자아이가 박수 치고 있다   The teacher is drawing a house on the blackboard. 선생님이 칠판에 집을 그리고 있다

06

There is an ice cream cone.

07

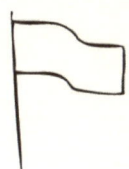

A flag flaps.

08

Her hair has curls.

09

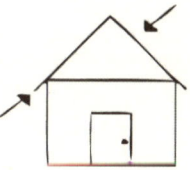

The house has a pointy roof.

10

There is a button down shirt.

Go on to the next step!

There is an ice cream cone. 아이스크림 콘이 있다   A flag flaps. 깃발이 펄럭인다   Her hair has curls. 그녀의 머리는 곱슬이다
The house has a pointy roof. 그 집은 지붕이 뾰족하다   There is a button down shirt. 단추가 달린 셔츠가 있다

step 04
START ...▶

01

A guy puts his finger on his head.

02

A person is coming down from the table.

03

A guy is packing a box.

04

A guy is counting the number with his fingers.

05

A person is sitting on the chair.

A guy puts his finger on his head. 한 남자가 손가락을 머리에 놓는다   A person is coming down from the table. 한 사람이 테이블에서 내려오고 있다   A guy is packing a box. 한 남자가 상자를 포장하고 있다   A guy is counting the number with his fingers. 한 남자가 손가락으로 수를 세고 있다   A person is sitting on the chair. 한 사람이 의자에 앉고 있다

06

A snake is sticking its tongue out.

07

There is an empty glass.

08

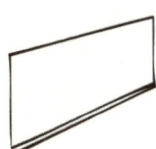

You need a chalk to write or draw something on the blackboard.

09

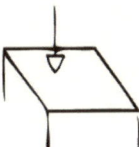

Put dishes on the table.

10

There is a circle.

Go on to the next step!

step 05

START ...▶

He is walking back and forth around the chair.

He is throwing away garbage into a trash can.

He is waving his hand to his friend.

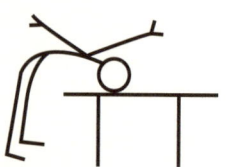

He hits the table with his head.

A girl is spinning around.

He is walking back and forth around the chair. 그가 의자 주위로 왔다 갔다 걷고 있다   He is throwing away garbage into a trash can. 그가 쓰레기를 쓰레기통에 버리고 있다   He is waving his hand to his friend. 그가 친구에게 손을 흔들고 있다   He hits the table with his head. 그가 머리로 테이블을 친다   A girl is spinning around. 여자아이가 돌고 있다

06

Orange is one of many kinds of fruits.

07

The place where people keep their money is a bank.

08

Each hand has five fingers.

09

The basket is empty.

10

There are countless stars in space.

Go on to the next step!

Orange is one of many kinds of fruits. 오렌지는 많은 종류의 과일 중 하나이다   The place where people keep their money is a bank. 사람들은 은행에 돈을 보관한다   Each hand has five fingers. 각 손에는 다섯 개의 손가락이 있다   The basket is empty. 그 바구니는 비어 있다   There are countless stars in space. 우주에는 셀 수 없이 많은 별들이 있다

step 06

START ···▶

01

Teacher wrote her name on the blackboard.

02

He is fat.

03

A guy is walking straight.

04

The guy takes something out of the box.

05

A guy is opening the door.

Teacher wrote her name on the blackboard. 선생님이 그녀의 이름을 칠판에 썼다   He is fat. 그는 뚱뚱하다   A guy is walking straight. 한 남자가 똑바로 걷고 있다   The guy takes something out of the box. 한 남자가 상자에서 무언가를 꺼낸다   A guy is opening the door. 한 남자가 문을 열고 있다

06

There is a pair of shoes.

07

A boy is opening his mouth.

08

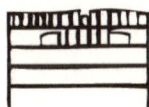

There are many books on the bookshelf.

09

Strawberry is one of many kinds of fruits.

10

Tuesday is marked on the timetable.

Go on to the next step!

There is a pair of shoes. 신발 한 켤레가 있다   A boy is opening his mouth. 남자아이가 입을 벌리고 있다   There are many books on the bookshelf. 책장에 많은 책들이 있다   Strawberry is one of many kinds of fruits. 딸기는 많은 과일 중 하나이다   Tuesday is marked on the timetable. 시간표에 화요일이 표시되어 있다

step 07
START ⋯▶

01

A guy is pointing at the ground.

02

The guy is supporting something over his head.

03

The guy is raising his arm up.

04

A person is picking up something off the table.

05

The guy is waving his hand to his friend.

A guy is pointing at the ground. 남자가 바닥을 가리키고 있다   The guy is supporting something over his head. 남자가 무언가를 머리 위로 받치고 있다   The guy is raising his arm up. 한 사내가 팔을 들고 있다   A person is picking up something off the table. 한 사람이 테이블에서 무언가를 집어 들고 있다   The guy is waving his hand to his friend. 한 사내가 그의 친구에게 손을 흔들고 있다

06

Every building has to have a window.

07

The place where people keep their money is a bank.

08

The trash can is empty.

09

There is nothing behind the table.

10

Each hand has five fingers.

Go on to the next step!

Every building has to have a window. 모든 건물에는 창문이 있어야 한다   The place where people keep their money is a bank. 사람들은 은행에 돈을 보관한다   The trash can is empty. 그 쓰레기통은 비어 있다   There is nothing behind the table. 테이블 뒤에 아무것도 없다   Each hand has five fingers. 각 손에는 다섯 개의 손가락이 있다

Lesson 1 **23**

step 08
START ...▶

01

A guy is standing up.

02

The guy is sitting on the table.

03

The guy is walking back and forth around the chair.

04

A person turns the light bulb on.

05

The guy is taking a deep breath.

A guy is standing up. 남자가 일어서고 있다   The guy is sitting on the table. 남자가 테이블 위에 앉아 있다   The guy is walking back and forth around the chair. 한 남자가 의자 주위를 왔다 갔다 걷고 있다   A person turns the light bulb on. 한 사람이 전구를 켠다   The guy is taking a deep breath. 한 사내가 크게 숨을 들이마시고 있다

06

Christians go to the church on Sundays.

07

The table has two legs.

08

The light bulb is on.

09

The girl is the daughter to the guy.

10

Fishes live under the water.

Go on to the next step!

Christians go to the church on Sundays. 기독교인들은 일요일마다 교회에 간다   The table has two legs. 그 테이블은 다리가 두 개 있다   The light bulb is on. 전구가 켜져 있다   The girl is the daughter to the guy. 그 여자아이는 남자의 딸이다   Fishes live under the water. 물고기들은 물에서 산다

Lesson 1 **25**

step 09
START ···▶

01

He is fat.

02

A guy is closing the door.

03

The guy is trying to turn the light bulb on.

04

A person is walking into the house.

05

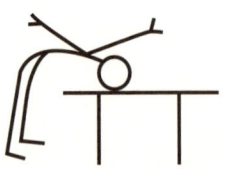

The guy is hitting the table with his head.

He is fat. 그는 뚱뚱하다   A guy is closing the door. 한 남자가 문을 닫고 있다   The guy is trying to turn the light bulb on. 한 남자가 전구를 켜려고 하고 있다.   A person is walking into the house. 한 사람이 집 안으로 걸어 들어가고 있다   The guy is hitting the table with his head. 한 사내가 머리로 테이블을 치고 있다

06

The door is closed.

07

Apple is delicious.

08

The boy has big ears.

09

Baseball is small and hard.

10

7

Go on to the next step!

Number seven is believed as a lucky number.

The door is closed. 문이 닫혀 있다   Apple is delicious. 사과는 맛있다   The boy has big ears. 소년은 큰 귀를 가지고 있다
Baseball is small and hard. 야구공은 작고 단단하다   Number seven is believed as a lucky number. 숫자 7은 행운의 숫자라고 믿어진다

step 10
START ...▶

01

A girl is writing on the blackboard.

02

The guy is flying.

03

A guy drops something into the box.

04

A person is sitting on the chair.

05

A guy steps into the trash can.

A girl is writing on the blackboard. 여자아이가 칠판에 글을 쓰고 있다   The guy is flying. 남자가 날고 있다   A guy drops something into the box. 한 남자가 뭔가를 상자 안에 떨어뜨린다   A person is sitting on the chair. 한 사람이 의자에 앉고 있다   A guy steps into the trash can. 한 사내가 쓰레기통에 발을 들여놓는다

06

The book is opened.

07

Cucumber is a kind of vegetable.

08

Pepper is used as a spice for many kinds of food.

09

A chair and a desk are combined.

10

A telephone, radio and photograph are on the desk.

Go on to the next Lesson!

The book is opened. 책이 펼쳐져 있다   Cucumber is a kind of vegetable. 오이는 채소 중 하나이다   Pepper is used as a spice for many kinds of food. 고추는 많은 음식에 양념으로 사용된다   A chair and a desk are combined. 의자와 책상이 붙어 있다   A telephone, radio and photograph are on the desk. 책상 위에 전화기, 라디오, 사진이 있다

Lesson 2

step II

START ⋯▶

01

A guy puts his finger on his head.

02

The man is lifting the chair

03

The guy takes something out of the box.

04

The teacher is drawing a house on the blackboard.

05

A guy is dancing with a girl.

A guy puts his finger on his head. 남자가 손가락을 머리 위에 놓고 있다   The man is lifting the chair 남자가 의자를 들어 올리고 있다   The guy takes something out of the box. 한 사내가 상자에서 무언가를 꺼낸다   The teacher is drawing a house on the blackboard. 선생님이 칠판에 집을 그리고 있다   A guy is dancing with a girl. 한 남자와 소녀가 춤을 추고 있다

오디오 QR 코드
Lesson 2

06

Pineapple is a tropical fruit.

07

People have to go to school.

08

The basket is empty.

09

The boy has his mouth opened.

10

10

Go on to the next step!

We use the decimal system.

Pineapple is a tropical fruit. 파인애플은 열대 과일이다   People have to go to school. 사람들은 학교에 가야 한다   The basket is empty. 그 바구니는 비어 있다   The boy has his mouth opened. 남자아이가 입을 벌리고 있다   We use the decimal system. 우리는 십진법을 사용한다

step 12
START ⋯▶

A guy is standing up.

A boy is cutting a paper.

The guy is stopping someone.

A guy is kneeling.

The guy is taking a deep breath.

A guy is standing up. 남자가 일어서고 있다   A boy is cutting a paper. 남자아이가 종이를 자르고 있다   The guy is stopping someone. 한 사내가 누군가를 멈춰 세우고 있다   A guy is kneeling. 사내가 무릎을 꿇고 있다   The guy is taking a deep breath. 한 사내가 크게 숨을 들이쉬고 있다

06

Cat is a popular pet.

07

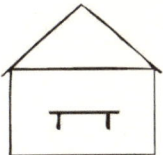

Restaurant sells food.

08

There is space between the two tables.

09

His arms are supporting something over his head.

10

People drink hot drinks with mug cups.

Go on to the next step!

Cat is a popular pet. 고양이는 인기 있는 애완동물이다   Restaurant sells food. 식당에선 음식을 판다   There is space between the two tables. 두 테이블 사이에 공간이 있다   His arms are supporting something over his head. 그의 두 팔이 머리 위로 무언가를 받치고 있다   People drink hot drinks with mug cups. 사람들은 머그컵으로 뜨거운 음료를 마신다

step 13
START ···▶

A boy is picking his ear.

A guy is pointing at the light bulb.

He is pointing at the ground.

A girl is turning the lever toward her.

A guy puts his arm down.

A boy is picking his ear. 남자아이가 귀를 후비고 있다 A guy is pointing at the light bulb. 사내가 전구를 가리키고 있다 He is pointing at the ground. 그는 바닥을 가리키고 있다 A girl is turning the lever toward her. 여자아이가 안쪽으로 레버를 돌리고 있다 A guy puts his arm down. 한 사내가 팔을 아래로 내린다

06

There is nothing underneath the table.

07

Westerners have a big nose.

08

There is a pair of shoes.

09

The cup is empty.

10

Thumb and Little finger are the smallest fingers among five fingers.

Go on to the next step!

There is nothing underneath the table. 테이블 밑에는 아무것도 없다   Westerners have a big nose. 서양인들은 코가 크다   There is a pair of shoes. 한 켤레의 신발이 있다   The cup is empty. 그 컵은 비어 있다   Thumb and Little finger are the smallest fingers among five fingers. 엄지와 새끼손가락은 다섯 손가락 중 가장 작다

step 14
START ···▶

01

He is waving his hand to his friend.

02

A guy is opening the door.

03

The guy is taking something out of the box.

04

The guy is pushing the table away.

05

The guy is lifting up the table.

He is waving his hand to his friend. 그가 친구에게 손을 흔들고 있다   A guy is opening the door. 사내가 문을 열고 있다   The guy is taking something out of the box. 사내가 상자에서 무언가를 꺼내고 있다   The guy is pushing the table away. 한 사내가 테이블을 밀어내고 있다   The guy is lifting up the table. 남자가 테이블을 들어 올리고 있다

06

There is a chair.

07

Thumb and ring finger are tied with strings.

08

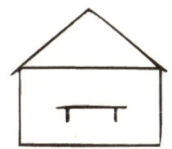

Restaurant sells food.

09

Every building must have a window.

10

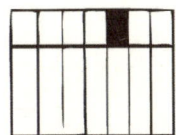

Go on to the next step!

Thursday is marked on the timetable.

There is a chair. 의자가 있다   Thumb and ring finger are tied with strings. 엄지와 넷째 손가락이 줄에 묶여 있다   Restaurant sells food. 식당에선 음식을 판다   Every building must have a window. 모든 건물들은 창문이 있어야 한다   Thursday is marked on the timetable. 시간표에 목요일이 표시되어 있다

step 15
START ···▶

<u>01</u>

The guy is lifting up the table.

<u>02</u>

A guy is stopping something (or someone).

<u>03</u>

A boy is going to school.

<u>04</u>

A person touches the chair.

<u>05</u>

A guy is turning the lever away from him.

The guy is lifting up the table. 남자가 테이블을 들어 올리고 있다   A guy is stopping something (or someone). 사내가 무언가(누군가)를 멈춰 세우고 있다   A boy is going to school. 남자아이가 학교에 가고 있다   A person touches the chair. 한 사람이 의자를 만진다
A guy is turning the lever away from him. 한 남자가 바깥쪽으로 레버를 돌리고 있다

06

A box is opened up.

07

The trash can is empty.

08

People have to go to school.

09

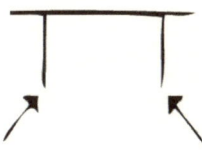

The table has two legs.

10

Everyone looks forward to Saturdays.

•••▶

Go on to the next step!

A box is opened up. 상자가 열려 있다   The trash can is empty. 쓰레기통은 비어 있다   People have to go to school. 사람들은 학교에 가야 한다.   The table has two legs. 테이블은 다리가 두 개다   Everyone looks forward to Saturdays. 모든 사람들이 토요일을 기대한다

step 16
START ...▶

A person is picking up something off the table.

02

He is fat.

03

The guy is supporting something over his head.

04

The guy is flying.

05

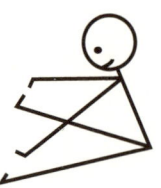

A boy is touching his toe.

A person is picking up something off the table. 한 사람이 테이블에서 무언가를 집어 올리고 있다 He is fat. 그는 뚱뚱하다 The guy is supporting something over his head. 한 사내가 머리 위로 무언가를 받치고 있다 The guy is flying. 사내가 날고 있다 A boy is touching his toe. 남자아이가 발가락을 만지고 있다

06

There is an ice cream cone.

07

Pencil has a pointy end.

08

Strawberry is one of many kinds of fruits.

09

The woman is mother to the boy.

10

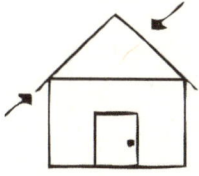

The house has a pointy roof.

Go on to the next step!

There is an ice cream cone. 아이스크림 콘이 있다   Pencil has a pointy end. 그 연필은 끝이 뾰족하다   Strawberry is one of many kinds of fruits. 딸기는 많은 과일 중 하나이다   The woman is mother to the boy. 그 여자는 남자아이의 어머니이다   The house has a pointy roof. 그 집은 지붕이 뾰족하다

step 17
START ···▶

The teacher is drawing a house on the blackboard.

A person touches the chair.

A girl is spinning around.

A boy is walking straight.

Two guys are shaking hands.

The teacher is drawing a house on the blackboard. 선생님이 칠판에 집을 그리고 있다   A person touches the chair. 한 사람이 의자를 만지고 있다   A girl is spinning around. 여자아이가 빙빙 돌고 있다   A boy is walking straight. 남자아이가 똑바로 걷고 있다   Two guys are shaking hands. 두 사람이 악수를 하고 있다

06

Hat helps to block the sunlight.

07

Pen has a pointy end.

08

Pear is a kind of fruit.

09

A snake is sticking its tongue out.

10

Go on to the next step!

Number four is believed as bad luck in Korea.

Hat helps to block the sunlight. 모자는 햇빛을 막는 데 도움을 준다   Pen has a pointy end. 펜은 끝이 뾰족하다   Pear is a kind of fruit. 배는 과일의 하나이다   A snake is sticking its tongue out. 뱀이 혀를 내밀고 있다   Number four is believed as bad luck in Korea. 숫자 4는 한국에서 불운으로 믿어진다

step 18
START ···▶

01

A guy is opening the door.

02

A guy is kneeling.

03

A boy is cutting a paper.

04

The man is lifting the chair.

05

A guy is dancing with a girl.

A guy is opening the door. 남자가 문을 열고 있다   A guy is kneeling. 남자가 무릎을 꿇고 있다   A boy is cutting a paper. 남자아이가 종이를 자르고 있다   The man is lifting the chair. 한 사내가 의자를 들어 올리고 있다   A guy is dancing with a girl. 남자가 여자아이와 춤을 추고 있다

06

Women's restroom is only for females.

07

Cat is a popular pet.

08

His arms are supporting something over his head.

09

The table on the left is smaller than the one on the right.

10

There are countless stars in space.

Go on to the next step!

step 19
START ⋯▶

The guy is trying to sit on the ground.

02

A boy is going to school.

03

A person is hiding under the table.

04

A boy is picking his ear.

05

A boy is taking his hat off.

The guy is trying to sit on the ground. 남자가 바닥에 앉으려 하고 있다   A boy is going to school. 남자아이가 학교에 가고 있다   A person is hiding under the table. 한 사람이 테이블 밑에 숨어 있다   A boy is picking his ear. 남자아이가 귀를 후비고 있다   A boy is taking his hat off. 남자아이가 모자를 벗고 있다

06

The place where people keep their money is a bank.

07

The basket is empty.

08

The boy has big ears.

09

Cat is a popular pet.

10

2

Chopsticks have to be in a pair.

Go on to the next step!

The place where people keep their money is a bank. 돈을 보관하는 곳은 은행이다   The basket is empty. 바구니는 비어 있다   The boy has big ears. 남자아이는 큰 귀를 가지고 있다   Cat is a popular pet. 고양이는 인기 있는 애완동물이다   Chopsticks have to be in a pair. 젓가락은 한 쌍이어야 한다

step 20
START ···▶

01

A boy is walking into the house.

02

The guy is flying.

03

A guy is standing up.

04

He is walking back and forth around the chair.

05

A boy is clapping.

A boy is walking into the house. 사내아이가 집 안으로 걸어 들어가고 있다　The guy is flying. 한 남자가 날고 있다　A guy is standing up. 한 남자가 일어서고 있다　He is walking back and forth around the chair. 그가 의자 주위를 왔다 갔다 하고 있다　A boy is clapping. 남자아이가 박수를 치고 있다

06

Christians go to the church on Sundays.

07

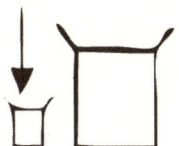

The box on the left is smaller than the one on the right.

08

Pineapple is a tropical fruit.

09

6

Dice have six sides.

10

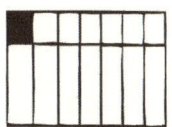

Everyone rests on Sundays.

Go on to the next Lesson!

Christians go to the church on Sundays. 기독교인들은 일요일마다 교회에 간다   The box on the left is smaller than the one on the right. 왼쪽 상자는 오른쪽 상자보다 작다   Pineapple is a tropical fruit. 파인애플은 열대 과일이다   Dice have six sides. 주사위는 면이 여섯 개이다   Everyone rests on Sundays. 모든 사람들은 일요일에 쉰다

Lesson 3

step 21

START ···▶

01

A guy puts his arm down.

02

A girl is writing on the blackboard.

03

The guy is supporting something over his head.

04

The teacher is drawing a house on the blackboard.

05

A person is coming down from the table.

A guy puts his arm down. 남자가 그의 팔을 내려놓는다   A girl is writing on the blackboard. 여자아이가 칠판에 글씨를 쓰고 있다
The guy is supporting something over his head. 한 사내가 머리 위로 무언가를 받치고 있다   The teacher is drawing a house on the blackboard. 선생님이 칠판에 집을 그리고 있다   A person is coming down from the table. 한 사람이 테이블에서 내려오고 있다

06

Strawberry is one of many kinds of fruits.

07

You need a chalk to write or draw something on the blackboard.

08

Men's room is only for males.

09

Pepper is used as a spice for many kinds of food.

10

Eyes are the most sensitive parts of the face.

Go on to the next step!

Strawberry is one of many kinds of fruits. 딸기는 많은 종류의 과일 중 하나이다   You need a chalk to write or draw something on the blackboard. 칠판에 무언가를 쓰거나 그리기 위해선 분필이 필요하다   Men's room is only for males. 남자 화장실은 남성 전용이다   Pepper is used as a spice for many kinds of food. 고추는 많은 음식에 양념으로 쓰인다   Eyes are the most sensitive parts of the face. 눈은 얼굴에서 가장 민감한 부분이다

step 22
START ...▶

A guy is closing the door.

02

The guy is pointing to the ground.

03

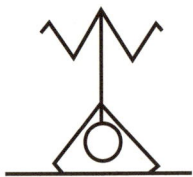

A guy is standing upside down.

04

The guy is taking a deep breath.

05

The guy is putting a box on the table.

A guy is closing the door. 한 사내가 문을 닫고 있다   The guy is pointing to the ground. 한 사내가 바닥을 가리키고 있다   A guy is standing upside down. 남자가 거꾸로 서 있다   The guy is taking a deep breath. 남자가 크게 숨을 들이쉬고 있다   The guy is putting a box on the table. 남자가 테이블 위에 상자를 놓고 있다

06

Pear is a kind of fruit.

07

Put that newspaper down on the right of the table.

08

A boy is opening his mouth.

09

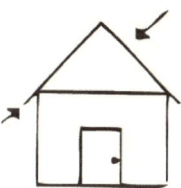

The house has a pointy roof.

10

The boy is pointing at his foot.

Go on to the next step!

Pear is a kind of fruit. 배는 과일의 한 종류이다   Put that newspaper down on the right of the table. 신문을 테이블 오른편에 내려놓아라   A boy is opening his mouth. 남자아이가 입을 벌리고 있다   The house has a pointy roof. 그 집은 지붕이 뾰족하다   The boy is pointing at his foot. 남자아이가 발을 가리키고 있다

Lesson 3 **53**

step 23
START ⋯▶

01

A girl is writing on the blackboard.

02

A person is sitting on the chair.

03

The guy is taking something out of the box.

04

A guy is opening the door.

05

A guy is standing upside down.

A girl is writing on the blackboard. 여자아이가 칠판에 글씨를 쓰고 있다   A person is sitting on the chair. 한 사람이 의자에 앉는다
The guy is taking something out of the box. 한 남자가 무언가를 상자 밖으로 꺼내고 있다   A guy is opening the door. 한 남자가 문을 열고 있다   A guy is standing upside down. 사내가 거꾸로 서 있다

06

There is space between the two tables.

07

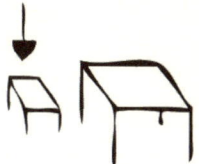

The table on the left is smaller than the one on the right.

08

There is an ice cream cone.

09

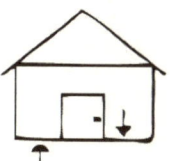

People come to the house in and out.

10

The girl is daughter to the man.

Go on to the next step!

There is space between the two tables. 두 테이블 사이에 공간이 있다　The table on the left is smaller than the one on the right. 왼쪽 테이블은 오른쪽 테이블보다 작다　There is an ice cream cone. 아이스크림 콘이 있다　People come to the house in and out. 사람들이 집 안팎으로 왔다 갔다 한다　The girl is daughter to the man. 그 여자아이는 그 남자의 딸이다

Lesson 3　**55**

step 24
START ...▶

01

The guy is stopping something (someone).

02

A guy is standing up.

03

A boy is taking his hat off.

04

The teacher is drawing a house on the blackboard.

05

A guy is lifting a girl over his head.

The guy is stopping something (someone). 남자가 무언가(누군가)를 멈춰 세우고 있다   A guy is standing up. 한 남자가 일어서고 있다   A boy is taking his hat off. 남자아이가 모자를 벗고 있다   The teacher is drawing a house on the blackboard. 선생님이 칠판에 집을 그리고 있다   A guy is lifting a girl over his head. 한 남자가 여자아이를 머리 위로 들어 올리고 있다

06

The light bulb is on.

07

The table has two legs.

08

Hospital is the place where treats sick people.

09

8

Octopus has eight legs.

10

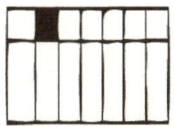

The new week starts on Monday.

Go on to the next step!

The light bulb is on. 전구가 켜져 있다 The table has two legs. 그 테이블은 다리가 두 개이다 Hospital is the place where treats sick people. 병원은 아픈 사람들을 치료하는 곳이다 Octopus has eight legs. 문어는 다리가 여덟 개이다 The new week starts on Monday. 새 주는 월요일에 시작된다

step 25
START ···▶

01

A guy is hitting the other guy's head.

02

He is throwing away garbage into a trash can.

03

A guy puts his finger on his head.

04

The guy is trying to turn the light bulb on.

05

A guy is packing a box.

A guy is hitting the other guy's head. 한 남자가 다른 남자의 머리를 때리고 있다   He is throwing away garbage into a trash can. 그가 쓰레기를 쓰레기통에 버리고 있다   A guy puts his finger on his head. 한 남자가 손가락을 머리에 대고 있다   The guy is trying to turn the light bulb on. 한 사내가 전구를 켜려 하고 있다   A guy is packing a box. 남자가 상자를 포장하고 있다

06

Christians go to the church on Sundays.

07

Westerners have a big nose.

08

A box is opened up.

09

The house on the right is smaller than the one on the left.

10

The boy has big ears.

● ● ● ▶

Go on to the next step!

Christians go to the church on Sundays. 기독교인들은 일요일마다 교회에 간다 Westerners have a big nose. 서양인들은 큰 코를 가지고 있다 A box is opened up. 상자가 열려 있다 The house on the right is smaller than the one on the left. 오른쪽 집이 왼쪽 집보다 작다 The boy has big ears. 소년은 큰 귀를 가지고 있다

step 26
START ∙∙∙▶

<u>01</u>

A guy is counting the number with his fingers.

<u>02</u>

Teacher wrote her name on the blackboard.

<u>03</u>

A person is hiding under the table.

<u>04</u>

A guy is standing up.

<u>05</u>

The guy is pushing the table away.

A guy is counting the number with his fingers. 남자가 손가락으로 수를 세고 있다   Teacher wrote her name on the blackboard. 선생님이 칠판에 그녀의 이름을 썼다   A person is hiding under the table. 한 사람이 테이블 아래에 숨어 있다   A guy is standing up. 남자가 일어서고 있다   The guy is pushing the table away. 한 사내가 테이블을 밀어내고 있다

06

Each hand has five fingers.

07

People drink hot drinks with mug cups.

08

Eyes are the most sensitive parts of the face.

09

Pen has a pointy end.

10

Go on to the next step!

Pepper is used as a spice for many kinds of food.

Each hand has five fingers. 각 손에는 다섯 개의 손가락이 있다   People drink hot drinks with mug cups. 사람들은 뜨거운 음료를 머그컵으로 마신다   Eyes are the most sensitive parts of the face. 눈은 얼굴에서 가장 민감한 부분이다   Pen has a pointy end. 펜은 끝이 뾰족하다   Pepper is used as a spice for many kinds of food. 고추는 많은 음식에 양념으로 사용된다

step 27
START ...▶

01

A guy puts his finger on his head.

02

A boy is cutting a paper.

03

The guy is running.

04

The man is smelling something on the table.

05

A boy is going to school.

A guy puts his finger on his head. 남자가 손가락을 머리에 놓는다   A boy is cutting a paper. 소년이 종이를 자르고 있다   The guy is running. 한 사내가 뛰어가고 있다   The man is smelling something on the table. 남자가 테이블 위 무언가의 냄새를 맡고 있다   A boy is going to school. 남자아이가 학교에 가고 있다

06

The light bulb is on.

07

Pineapple is a tropical fruit.

08

The boy has big ears.

09

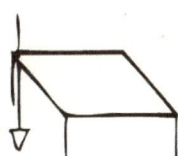

Put a chair on the left of the table.

10

Fish lives under the water.

Go on to the next step!

step 28
START ...▶

01

A guy is standing up.

02

A guy is opening the door.

03

The guy is lifting up the table.

04

A person is picking up something off the table.

05

He is walking back and forth around the chair.

A guy is standing up. 남자가 일어서고 있다 A guy is opening the door. 한 사내가 문을 열고 있다 The guy is lifting up the table. 한 남자가 테이블을 들어 올리고 있다 A person is picking up something off the table. 한 사람이 테이블에서 무언가를 집어 올리고 있다 He is walking back and forth around the chair. 그가 의자 주위를 왔다 갔다 하고 있다

06

Hat helps to block the sunlight.

07

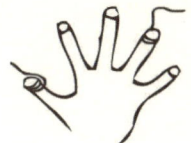

Thumb and ring finger are tied with strings.

08

9

Baseball has nine innings.

09

The man and woman are parents to the boy.

10

Key locks and unlocks a lock or a door.

Go on to the next step!

step 29
START ···▶

A guy is pointing at the light bulb.

Two guys are exchanging a high five.

Teacher wrote her name on the blackboard.

A guy is packing a box.

The guy is hitting the table with his head.

A guy is pointing at the light bulb. 남자가 전구를 가리키고 있다   Two guys are exchanging a high five. 두 남자가 하이파이브를 하고 있다   Teacher wrote her name on the blackboard. 선생님이 그녀의 이름을 칠판에 썼다   A guy is packing a box. 남자가 상자를 포장하고 있다   The guy is hitting the table with his head. 한 사내가 머리로 테이블을 치고 있다

06

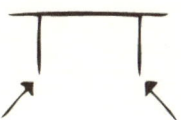

The table has two legs.

07

Knife is used to cut things.

08

Apple is delicious.

09

The house has pointy roof.

10

The boy is brother to the girl.

Go on to the next step!

The table has two legs. 그 테이블은 다리가 두 개다   Knife is used to cut things. 칼은 물건들을 자르는 데 사용된다   Apple is delicious. 사과는 맛있다   The house has pointy roof. 그 집은 지붕이 뾰족하다   The boy is brother to the girl. 그 소년은 여자아이의 남자 형제이다

Lesson 3 **67**

step 30
START ...▶

01

The teacher is drawing a house on the blackboard.

02

The boy is picking his ear.

03

A boy is walking into the house.

04

The guy is putting a box on the table.

05

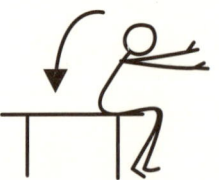

The guy is sitting on the table.

The teacher is drawing a house on the blackboard. 선생님이 칠판에 집을 그리고 있다   The boy is picking his ear. 소년이 귀를 후비고 있다   A boy is walking into the house. 남자아이가 집 안으로 걸어 들어가고 있다   The guy is putting a box on the table. 한 남자가 테이블 위에 상자를 놓는다   The guy is sitting on the table. 한 사내가 테이블 위에 앉아 있다

06

The basket is empty.

07

Wine is made of grapes.

08

A chair and a desk are combined.

09

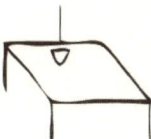

Put the dishes down on the table.

10

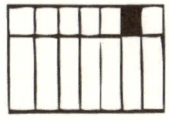

Friday the thirteenth is believed as a unlucky day in some countries.

Go on to the next Lesson!

The basket is empty. 그 바구니는 비어 있다   Wine is made of grapes. 와인은 포도로 만들어진다   A chair and a desk are combined. 의자와 책상이 붙어 있다   Put the dishes down on the table. 접시들을 테이블 위에 내려놓아라   Friday the thirteenth is believed as a unlucky day in some countries. 13일의 금요일은 몇몇 나라에서 불길한 날로 믿어지고 있다

Lesson 4

step 31

START ···▶

01

The guy is lifting up the table.

02

A guy is counting the number with his fingers.

03

The guy is pushing the table away.

04

A guy puts his finger on his head.

05

The guy is kicking his leg.

The guy is lifting up the table. 남자가 테이블을 들어 올리고 있다   A guy is counting the number with his fingers. 한 사내가 손가락으로 수를 세고 있다   The guy is pushing the table away. 남자가 테이블을 밀어내고 있다   A guy puts his finger on his head. 남자가 손가락을 머리에 놓는다   The guy is kicking his leg. 남자가 다리를 차고 있다

06

There is an ice cream cone.

07

Pencil has a pointy end.

08

His arms are supporting something over his head.

09

Men's room is only for males.

10

Cucumber is a kind of vegetable.

Go on to the next step!

There is an ice cream cone. 아이스크림 콘이 있다   Pencil has a pointy end. 연필은 끝이 뾰족하다   His arms are supporting something over his head. 그의 팔이 머리 위로 무언가를 받치고 있다   Men's room is only for males. 남자 화장실은 남성 전용이다
Cucumber is a kind of vegetable. 오이는 야채의 하나이다

step 32
START ...▶

01

The guy is pointing at the ground.

02

The teacher is drawing a house on the blackboard.

03

A boy is putting his hat on.

04

The man is smelling something on the table.

05

A guy is closing the door.

The guy is pointing at the ground. 남자가 바닥을 가리키고 있다   The teacher is drawing a house on the blackboard. 선생님이 칠판에 집을 그리고 있다   A boy is putting his hat on. 소년이 모자를 쓰고 있다   The man is smelling something on the table. 한 남자가 테이블 위 무언가의 냄새를 맡고 있다   A guy is closing the door. 남자가 문을 닫고 있다

06

Clock has an hour hand, a minute hand and a second hand.

07

Spider has eight legs.

08

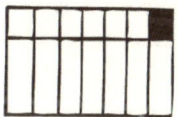

Everyone looks forward to Saturdays.

09

Eyes are the most sensitive parts of the face.

10

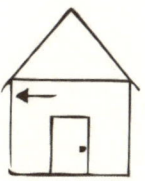

The house has four walls.

••• ▶

Go on to the next step!

Clock has an hour hand, a minute hand and a second hand. 시계에는 시침, 분침, 초침이 있다   Spider has eight legs. 거미는 다리가 여덟 개이다   Everyone looks forward to Saturdays. 모든 사람들이 토요일을 기대한다   Eyes are the most sensitive parts of the face. 눈은 얼굴에서 가장 민감한 부분이다   The house has four walls. 집은 사면이 벽이다

step 33
START ...▶

01

A person touches the chair.

02

The boy is walking out of the house.

03

Two guys are shaking hands.

04

A guy is yelling.

05

A guy is dancing with a girl.

A person touches the chair 한 사람이 의자를 만진다   The boy is walking out of the house. 남자아이가 집 밖으로 걸어 나오고 있다   Two guys are shaking hands. 두 사람이 악수를 하고 있다   A guy is yelling. 한 남자가 고함을 지르고 있다   A guy is dancing with a girl. 한 남자와 소녀가 춤을 추고 있다

06

Dog is a popular pet.

07

People have to go to school.

08

Clock has an hour hand, a minute hand and a second hand.

09

7

Number seven is believed as a lucky number.

10

The woman is grandmother to the girl.

Go on to the next step!

Dog is a popular pet. 개는 인기 있는 애완동물이다   People have to go to school. 사람들은 학교에 가야 한다   Clock has an hour hand, a minute hand and a second hand. 시계에는 시침, 분침, 초침이 있다   Number seven is believed as a lucky number. 숫자 7은 행운의 숫자로 믿어진다   The woman is grandmother to the girl. 여자는 소녀의 할머니이다

step 34
START ···▶

01

A person is sitting on the chair.

02

A guy steps into the trash can.

03

A girl is turning the lever toward her.

04

A guy is packing a box.

05

A girl is crossing her arms.

A person is sitting on the chair. 한 사람이 의자에 앉는다   A guy steps into the trash can. 남자가 쓰레기통에 발을 넣고 있다   A girl is turning the lever toward her. 여자아이가 안쪽으로 레버를 돌리고 있다   A guy is packing a box. 한 사내가 상자를 포장하고 있다   A girl is crossing her arms. 여자아이가 팔을 교차시키고 있다

06

Each hand has five fingers.

07

Pen has a pointy end.

08

The lady's hair has curls.

09

Westerners have a big nose.

10

The trash can is empty.

Go on to the next step!

Each hand has five fingers. 각각의 손에는 손가락이 다섯 개 있다   Pen has a pointy end. 펜은 끝이 뾰족하다   The lady's hair has curls. 여자의 머리는 곱슬이다   Westerners have a big nose. 서양인들은 코가 크다   The trash can is empty. 그 쓰레기통은 비어 있다

step 35
START ···▶

01

A guy is opening the door.

02

He is throwing away garbage into a trash can.

03

A person is hiding under the table.

04

The guy is taking a deep breath.

05

The guy is running.

A guy is opening the door. 사내가 문을 열고 있다   He is throwing away garbage into a trash can. 그가 쓰레기를 쓰레기통에 버리고 있다   A person is hiding under the table. 한 사람이 테이블 밑에 숨어 있다   The guy is taking a deep breath. 사내가 크게 숨을 들이쉬고 있다   The guy is running. 사내가 뛰어가고 있다

06

The book is opened.

07

There are countless stars in space.

08

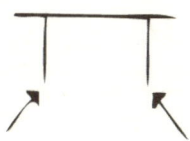

The table has two legs.

09

Car is a type of transportation.

10

9

Go on to the next step!

Baseball has nine innings.

The book is opened. 책이 펼쳐져 있다   There are countless stars in space. 우주에는 셀 수 없이 많은 별이 있다   The table has two legs. 그 테이블은 다리가 두 개이다   Car is a type of transportation. 자동차는 운송 수단의 하나이다   Baseball has nine innings. 야구는 9회까지 있다

step 36
START ...▶

01
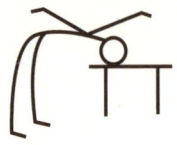

The guy is hitting the table with his head.

02

The guy is raising both his arms up.

03

The guy is trying to turn the light bulb on.

04

The guy puts his arm down.

05

The guy is stopping something (someone).

The guy is hitting the table with his head. 남자가 머리로 테이블을 치고 있다   The guy is raising both his arms up. 사내가 두 팔을 높이 들고 있다   The guy is trying to turn the light bulb on. 한 남자가 전구를 켜려 하고 있다   The guy puts his arm down. 남자가 팔을 내려놓는다   The guy is stopping something (someone). 한 남자가 무언가(누군가)를 멈춰 세우고 있다

06

A flag flaps.

07

The boy's head is shaved.

08

The man and woman are parents to the boy and girl.

09

5

Each hand and foot has five fingers and toes.

10

People buy things with money.

Go on to the next step!

step 37

START ⋯▶

01

A person is sitting on the chair.

02

The guy is taking something out of the box.

03

The guy is stopping something (someone).

04

A boy is picking his ear.

05

A guy is yelling.

A person is sitting on the chair. 한 사람이 의자에 앉는다   The guy is taking something out of the box. 남자가 상자에서 무언가를 꺼내고 있다   The guy is stopping something (someone). 한 사내가 무언가(누군가)를 멈춰 세우고 있다   A boy is picking his ear. 남자아이가 귀를 후비고 있다   A guy is yelling. 남자가 고함을 지르고 있다

06

Frog can live under the water and on land.

07

Clock has an hour hand, a minute hand and a second hand.

08

Apple is delicious.

09

The basket is empty.

10

There is nothing under the table.

Go on to the next step!

Frog can live under the water and on land. 개구리는 물과 땅에서 살 수 있다   Clock has an hour hand, a minute hand and a second hand. 시계에는 시침, 분침, 초침이 있다   Apple is delicious. 사과는 맛있다   The basket is empty. 그 바구니는 비어 있다
There is nothing under the table. 테이블 밑에는 아무것도 없다

Lesson 4 **83**

step 38
START ···▶

01

The teacher is drawing a house on the blackboard.

02

The guy is pointing at the ground.

03

A guy is kneeling.

04

He is waving his hand at his friend.

05

A girl is crossing her arms.

The teacher is drawing a house on the blackboard. 선생님이 칠판에 집을 그리고 있다   The guy is pointing at the ground. 남자가 바닥을 가리키고 있다   A guy is kneeling. 한 남자가 무릎을 꿇고 있다   He is waving his hand at his friend. 그가 친구에게 손을 흔들고 있다   A girl is crossing her arms. 여자아이가 팔을 교차시키고 있다

06

20

Twenty Questions is a popular game among children.

07

Spider has 8 legs.

08

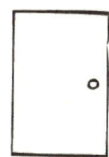

The door has a doorknob.

09

The house on the right is smaller than the one on the left.

10

The girl is daughter to the man.

Go on to the next step!

Twenty Questions is a popular game among children. 스무고개는 어린이들에게 인기 있는 놀이이다   Spider has 8 legs. 거미는 다리가 여덟 개이다   The door has a doorknob. 그 문은 손잡이가 있다   The house on the right is smaller than the one on the left. 오른쪽 집이 왼쪽 집보다 작다   The girl is daughter to the man. 여자아이는 그 남자의 딸이다

Lesson 4 **85**

step 39
START ··· ▶

01

A guy is pointing at the light bulb.

02

The guy takes something out of the box.

03

A guy is opening the door.

04

Teacher wrote her name on the blackboard.

05

The guy is pushing the table away.

A guy is pointing at the light bulb. 남자가 전구를 가리키고 있다   The guy takes something out of the box. 남자가 상자에서 무언가를 꺼낸다   A guy is opening the door. 사내가 문을 열고 있다   Teacher wrote her name on the blackboard. 선생님이 그녀의 이름을 칠판에 썼다   The guy is pushing the table away. 남자가 테이블을 밀어내고 있다

06

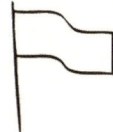

The flag is flapping.

07

People have to go to school.

08

7

Number seven is believed as a lucky number in many countries.

09

The boy is pointing at his foot.

10

Fishes live under the water.

Go on to the next step!

The flag is flapping. 깃발이 펄럭이고 있다   People have to go to school. 사람들은 학교에 가야 한다   Number seven is believed as a lucky number in many countries. 숫자 7은 많은 나라에서 행운의 숫자로 믿어진다   The boy is pointing at his foot. 소년이 발을 가리키고 있다   Fishes live under the water. 물고기들은 물에서 산다

step 40
START ···▶

<u>01</u>

The guy puts his arm down.

<u>02</u>

The guy is running.

<u>03</u>

The guy is trying to sit on the ground.

<u>04</u>

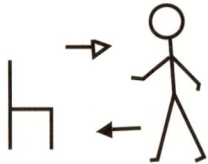

He is walking back and forth around the chair.

<u>05</u>

A guy is turning the lever away from him.

The guy puts his arm down. 남자가 팔을 내린다   The guy is running. 남자가 달리고 있다   The guy is trying to sit on the ground. 사내가 바닥에 앉으려고 한다   He is walking back and forth around the chair. 그가 의자 주위를 왔다 갔다 하고 있다   A guy is turning the lever away from him. 남자가 바깥쪽으로 레버를 돌리고 있다

06

New week starts on Monday.

07

Thumb and little finger are the smallest fingers among five fingers.

08

The table has two legs.

09

Men's room is only for males.

10

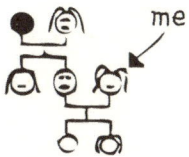

The man is father-in-law to the woman.

Go on to the next step!

New week starts on Monday. 새로운 주가 월요일에 시작된다   Thumb and little finger are the smallest fingers among five fingers. 엄지와 새끼 손가락은 다섯 손가락 중 가장 작다   The table has two legs. 그 테이블은 다리가 두 개이다   Men's room is only for males. 남자 화장실은 남성 전용이다   The man is father-in-law to the woman. 그 남자는 그 여자의 시아버지이다

step 41
START ...▶

He is throwing away garbage into a trash can.

02

A boy is going to school.

03

He is fat.

04

A guy is counting the number with his fingers.

05

The guy is trying to turn the light bulb on.

He is throwing away garbage into a trash can. 그가 쓰레기를 쓰레기통에 버리고 있다   A boy is going to school. 소년이 학교에 가고 있다   He is fat. 그는 뚱뚱하다   A guy is counting the number with his fingers. 한 남자가 손가락으로 수를 세고 있다   The guy is trying to turn the light bulb on. 남자가 전구를 켜려 하고 있다

06

The book is opened.

07

Wine is made of grapes.

08

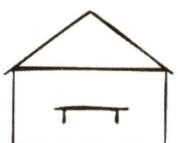

Restaurant sells food.

09

4

Number four is believed as bad luck in some Asian countries.

10

Go on to the next step!

Baseball is small and hard.

The book is opened. 책이 펼쳐져 있다   Wine is made of grapes. 와인은 포도로 만들어진다   Restaurant sells food. 식당에선 음식을 판다   Number four is believed as bad luck in some Asian countries. 숫자 4는 몇몇 아시아 국가에서 불운으로 믿어진다
Baseball is small and hard. 야구공은 작고 단단하다

step 42

START ...▶

01

The guy is flying.

02

A guy drops something into the box.

03

A guy is kneeling.

04

A boy is putting a hat on.

05

A guy is lifting a girl over his head.

The guy is flying. 남자가 날고 있다 A guy drops something into the box. 한 사내가 무언가를 상자 안에 떨어뜨린다 A guy is kneeling. 한 사내가 무릎을 꿇고 있다 A boy is putting a hat on. 남자아이가 모자를 쓰고 있다 A guy is lifting a girl over his head. 한 남자가 여자아이를 머리 위로 들어 올리고 있다

06

The box is opened up.

07

10

We use the decimal system.

08

The man is grandfather to the boy.

09

Orange skin is rough.

10

A telephone, radio and a photograph are on the desk.

Go on to the next Chapter!

The box is opened up. 그 상자는 열려 있다   We use the decimal system. 우리는 십진법을 사용한다   The man is grandfather to the boy. 남자는 소년의 할아버지이다   Orange skin is rough. 오렌지 껍질은 거칠다   A telephone, radio and a photograph are on the desk. 책상 위에 전화기, 라디오, 사진이 있다

ENGLISH
ICEBREAK

CHAPTER 2

Lesson 5 - 8   Graphic Sheets 2

Lesson 5

step 01

START ⋯▶

01

The guy is scratching his head.

02

The guy is lifting the table up.

03

The guy hits the table with his head.

04

A boy puts his hat on.

05

Two guys are exchanging a high-five.

The guy is scratching his head. 남자가 머리를 긁적이고 있다   The guy is lifting the table up. 남자가 테이블을 들어 올리고 있다
The guy hits the table with his head. 남자가 머리로 테이블을 친다   A boy puts his hat on. 남자아이가 모자를 쓴다   Two guys are exchanging a high-five. 두 사람이 하이파이브를 한다

06

A guy is pushing the table.

07

Library loans out the books to people.

08

Goblet has a stem and base but no handle.

09

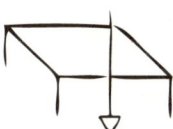

Put a chair in front of the table.

10

18

In America, when a person is eighteen, he or she is treated as an adult.

Go on to the next step!

A guy is pushing the table. 남자가 테이블을 밀고 있다   Library loans out the books to people. 도서관은 사람들에게 책을 빌려 준다
Goblet has a stem and base but no handle. 포도주잔은 굽과 받침이 있고 손잡이가 없다   Put a chair in front of the table. 테이블 앞에
의자를 놓아라   In America, when a person is eighteen, he or she is treated as an adult. 미국에선 18살이면 성인 대우를 받는다

step 02
START ···▶

01

A person is praying.

02

The guy is stuck under the table.

03

A girl is dancing.

04

A guy is eating an ice cream cone.

05

A guy is wiping the window with a cloth.

A person is praying. 한 사람이 기도를 하고 있다　The guy is stuck under the table. 남자가 책상 밑에 갇혀 있다　A girl is dancing. 여자아이가 춤을 추고 있다　A guy is eating an ice cream cone. 남자가 아이스크림 콘을 먹고 있다　A guy is wiping the window with a cloth. 남자가 걸레로 창문을 닦고 있다

06

A boy is clapping.

07

Time is valuable.

08

Wine is made of grapes.

09

Movie house shows the movies.

10

14

February 14th is Valentine's Day.

Go on to the next step!

A boy is clapping. 남자아이가 손뼉을 치고 있다   Time is valuable. 시간은 소중하다   Wine is made of grapes. 와인은 포도로 만들어진다   Movie house shows the movies. 영화관에선 영화를 보여 준다   February 14th is Valentine's Day. 2월 14일은 밸런타인데이이다

step 03
START ⋯▶

<u>01</u>

The guy is stopping something (someone).

<u>02</u>

The guy is trying to balance on the table.

<u>03</u>

A guy is going up the stairs.

<u>04</u>

A boy is stretching his leg.

<u>05</u>

A guy raises his hand.

The guy is stopping something (someone). 남자가 무언가(누군가)를 멈춰 세우고 있다   The guy is trying to balance on the table. 남자가 테이블 위에서 중심을 잡으려 하고 있다   A guy is going up the stairs. 한 남자가 계단을 오르고 있다   A boy is stretching his leg. 남자아이가 다리를 스트레칭하고 있다   A guy raises his hand. 한 사내가 손을 든다

06

A guy is holding a picture on his hand.

07

Supermarket sells groceries, snacks, drinks and so on.

08

Cat is one of the most popular pets.

09

Legs support one's weight.

10

Spoon is used to eat food.

Go on to the next step!

A guy is holding a picture on his hand. 남자가 손에 사진을 들고 있다   Supermarket sells groceries, snacks, drinks and so on. 슈퍼마켓에선 식품, 과자, 음료 등을 판매한다   Cat is one of the most popular pets. 고양이는 가장 인기 있는 애완동물들 중 하나이다   Legs support one's weight. 다리는 사람의 무게를 지탱한다   Spoon is used to eat food. 숟가락은 음식을 먹을 때 사용된다

step 04
START ...▶

01

A boy is putting on a hat.

02

A guy is drinking water.

03

A guy is climbing down the ladder.

04

A person is washing his(her) hands with water.

05

A girl is writing her name on the blackboard.

A boy is putting on a hat. 남자아이가 모자를 쓰고 있다   A guy is drinking water. 남자가 물을 마시고 있다   A guy is climbing down the ladder. 남자가 사다리를 내려오고 있다   A person is washing his(her) hands with water. 한 사람이 물로 손을 씻고 있다
A girl is writing her name on the blackboard. 여자아이가 칠판에 이름을 쓰고 있다

06

A guy is holding his hand up.

07

A boy is pointing at his foot.

08

There is a napkin next to the fork.

09

20

Twenty Questions is a popular game among children.

10

The flashlight is portable.

Go on to the next step!

A guy is holding his hand up. 남자가 손을 들고 있다 A boy is pointing at his foot. 남자아이가 발을 가리키고 있다 There is a napkin next to the fork. 냅킨은 포크 옆에 있다 Twenty Questions is a popular game among children. 스무고개는 아이들 사이에서 인기 있는 놀이이다 The flashlight is portable. 손전등은 휴대가 가능하다

step 05
START ⋯▶

The guy is jumping.

02

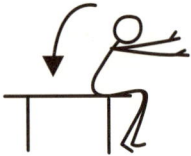

A guy lies down on the table.

03

A guy is lighting the candles.

04

A guy is squeezing the newspaper.

05

A guy is sleeping on the floor.

The guy is jumping. 남자가 점프를 하고 있다   A guy lies down on the table. 한 남자가 테이블 위에 눕는다   A guy is lighting the candles. 한 사내가 촛불을 켜고 있다   A guy is squeezing the newspaper. 남자가 신문을 꽉 쥐고 있다   A guy is sleeping on the floor. 남자가 바닥에서 잠을 자고 있다

06

A couple is kissing.

07

Women's restroom is only for females.

08

Pear is a kind of fruit.

09

The flag is flapping.

10

The man and woman are parents to the children.

Go on to the next step!

A couple is kissing. 한 커플이 키스를 하고 있다   Women's restroom is only for females. 여자 화장실은 여성 전용이다   Pear is a kind of fruit. 배는 과일의 일종이다   The flag is flapping. 깃발이 펄럭이고 있다   The man and woman are parents to the children. 남자와 여자는 그 아이들의 부모다

step 06
START ...▶

01

A boy is taking his hat off.

02

A guy is wiping the window with a cloth.

03

A guy hits the table with his head.

04

A guy lies down on the bed.

05

A guy is closing a small box.

A boy is taking his hat off. 남자아이가 모자를 벗고 있다 A guy is wiping the window with a cloth. 남자가 걸레로 창문을 닦고 있다
A guy hits the table with his head. 남자가 머리로 테이블을 친다 A guy lies down on the bed. 한 남자가 침대 위에 눕는다 A guy is closing a small box. 남자가 작은 상자를 닫고 있다

06

A guy pours trash out on the table.

07

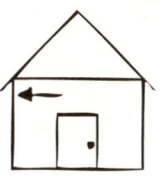

The house has 4 walls.

08

The girl is daughter to the woman.

09

People put money in a bank.

10

Fish lives under the water.

Go on to the next step!

A guy pours trash out on the table. 남자가 테이블 위에 쓰레기를 붓는다   The house has 4 walls. 그 집은 사면이 벽이다   The girl is daughter to the woman. 소녀는 그 여자의 딸이다   People put money in a bank. 사람들은 은행에 예금을 한다   Fish lives under the water. 물고기는 물에서 산다

step 07
START ···▶

01

A guy chugs the water.

02

A guy whistles a song.

03

Two guys are shaking hands.

04

A boy is sticking his tongue out.

05

A boy is combing his hair.

A guy chugs the water. 남자가 물을 단숨에 들이킨다   A guy whistles a song. 한 남자가 휘파람으로 노래를 부른다   Two guys are shaking hands. 두 남자가 악수를 하고 있다   A boy is sticking his tongue out. 남자아이가 혀를 내밀고 있다   A boy is combing his hair. 남자아이가 머리를 빗고 있다

06

A guy is going up the stairs.

07

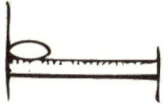

Bed is where people sleep.

08

Food is put on the plate.

09

10

People have ten fingers and ten toes.

10

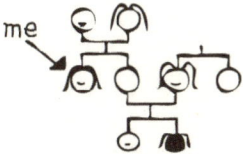

The girl is niece to the woman.

Go on to the next step!

A guy is going up the stairs. 남자가 계단을 오르고 있다 Bed is where people sleep. 침대는 사람들이 자는 곳이다 Food is put on the plate. 음식은 접시 위에 놓인다 People have ten fingers and ten toes. 사람들은 열 개의 손가락과 발가락을 가지고 있다 The girl is niece to the woman. 여자아이는 여자의 조카(여자)이다

Lesson 5 **109**

step 08

START ···▶

01 The lady winks with her left eye.

02 The guy is trying to stand up on the chair.

03 A guy raises his arm.

04 A boy is pouring the water into the glass.

05 The guy is scratching his head.

The lady winks with her left eye. 여자가 왼쪽 눈으로 윙크한다   The guy is trying to stand up on the chair. 남자가 의자 위에 올라서려 하고 있다   A guy raises his arm. 한 남자가 손을 든다   A boy is pouring the water into the glass. 남자아이가 잔에 물을 따르고 있다   The guy is scratching his head. 남자가 머리를 긁적이고 있다

06

A boy is hiding behind the box.

07

Movie house shows the movies.

08

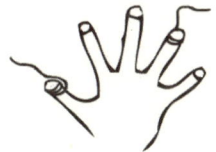

Thumb and ring finger are tied to strings.

09

A girl is wearing a skirt.

10

20

Go on to the next step!

Last century was the 20th century.

A boy is hiding behind the box. 남자아이가 상자 뒤에 숨어 있다   Movie house shows the movies. 영화관은 영화를 보여 준다
Thumb and ring finger are tied to strings. 엄지와 넷째 손가락이 줄에 묶여 있다   A girl is wearing a skirt. 여자아이가 치마를 입고 있다   Last century was the 20th century. 지난 세기는 20세기였다

step 09
START ...▶

01

A guy is running fast.

02

A lady opens her mouth.

03

A girl has her arms crossed.

04

A boy takes off his hat.

05

A guy is raising his leg.

A guy is running fast. 남자가 빠르게 달리고 있다   A lady opens her mouth. 여자가 입을 벌린다   A girl has her arms crossed. 여자아이가 팔을 교차하고 있다   A boy takes off his hat. 남자아이가 모자를 벗는다   A guy is raising his leg. 남자가 다리를 올리고 있다

06

A guy pours trash out on the table.

07

Bottle is recyclable.

08

Show me your back.

09

The house has 4 walls.

10

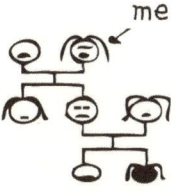

The girl is granddaughter to the woman.

Go on to the next step!

A guy pours trash out on the table. 남자가 테이블 위에 쓰레기를 쏟는다   Bottle is recyclable. 병은 재활용할 수 있다   Show me your back. 너의 등을 보여 줘   The house has 4 walls. 그 집은 사면이 벽이다   The girl is granddaughter to the woman. 여자아이는 그 여자의 손녀이다

step 10
START ···▶

01

A boy is clapping his hands.

02

A guy is closing a small box.

03

A girl is stretching her arms out.

04

A guy is showing a picture.

05

A girl is turning around.

A boy is clapping his hands. 남자아이가 손뼉을 치고 있다   A guy is closing a small box. 남자가 작은 상자를 닫고 있다   A girl is stretching her arms out. 소녀가 팔을 뻗고 있다   A guy is showing a picture. 남자가 사진을 보여 주고 있다   A girl is turning around. 여자아이가 돌고 있다

06

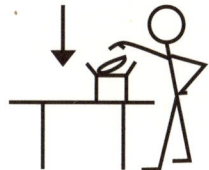

A guy drops a cucumber into the box.

07

Fork is used to eat food.

08

There are eggs in the basket.

09

5

In basketball, five players from each team play on the court.

10

Go on to the next Lesson!

Many people read a newspaper everyday.

A guy drops a cucumber into the box. 남자가 상자에 오이를 떨어뜨린다   Fork is used to eat food. 포크는 음식을 먹는 데 쓰인다
There are eggs in the basket. 계란이 바구니 안에 있다   In basketball, five players from each team play on the court. 농구에선 각 팀 선수 5명이 코트에서 경기를 한다   Many people read a newspaper everyday. 많은 사람들이 매일 신문을 읽는다

Lesson 6

step ll

START ···▶

01

A boy is wearing a hat.

02

A guy is coming down from the table.

03

Two guys are exchanging a high-five.

04

A boy is combing his hair.

05

A guy pours trashes out on the table.

A boy is wearing a hat. 남자아이가 모자를 쓰고 있다   A guy is coming down from the table. 남자가 테이블에서 내려오고 있다
Two guys are exchanging a high-five. 두 남자가 하이파이브를 하고 있다   A boy is combing his hair. 소년이 머리를 빗고 있다   A guy pours trashes out on the table. 한 남자가 테이블 위에 쓰레기를 쏟는다

06

A guy is picking up the cucumber from the floor.

07

Goblet has a stem and base but no handle.

08

Girls wear blouses.

09

It's a picture of a guy.

10

 Go on to the next step!

When two people get married, they become a husband and wife.

A guy is picking up the cucumber from the floor. 남자가 바닥에서 오이를 집어 올리고 있다   Goblet has a stem and base but no handle. 포도주잔은 굽과 받침이 있으며 손잡이가 없다   Girls wear blouses. 여자들은 블라우스를 입는다   It's a picture of a guy. 그것은 한 남자의 사진이다   When two people get married, they become a husband and wife. 두 사람이 결혼하면, 그들은 남편과 아내가 된다

step 12
START ...▶

01

A girl has her arms crossed.

02

A guy is wiping the window with a cloth.

03

The guy is trying to stand up on the chair.

04

A guy is sweeping the floor with a broom.

05

The lady winks with her left eye.

A girl has her arms crossed. 여자아이가 팔을 교차시키고 있다   A guy is wiping the window with a cloth. 남자가 걸레로 창문을 닦고 있다   The guy is trying to stand up on the chair. 남자가 의자 위에 올라서려 하고 있다   A guy is sweeping the floor with a broom. 사내가 빗자루로 바닥을 쓸고 있다   The lady winks with her left eye. 여자가 왼쪽 눈으로 윙크한다

06

A girl is turning the lever toward her.

07

The ruler is used for measuring the length of things.

08

We can see ourselves on a mirror because a mirror reflects the light.

09

Put a chair in front of the table.

10

17

Seventeen is a very popular magazine among American teenaged girls.

•••▶

Go on to the next step!

A girl is turning the lever toward her. 여자아이가 자기 쪽으로 레버를 돌리고 있다   The ruler is used for measuring the length of things. 자는 물건의 길이를 잴 때 사용된다   We can see ourselves on a mirror because a mirror reflects the light. 거울은 빛을 반사시키기 때문에 우리는 거울로 자기 자신을 볼 수 있다   Put a chair in front of the table. 의자를 테이블 앞에 놓아라   Seventeen is a very popular magazine among American teenaged girls. *세븐틴*은 미국 십대 소녀들 사이에서 굉장히 인기 있는 잡지이다

Lesson 6 **119**

step 13
START ••▶

A guy is eating an ice cream cone.

02

A girl is stretching her arms out.

03

The guy is trying to stand up on the chair.

04

The guy is jumping.

05

A boy is pulling a girl's hair.

A guy is eating an ice cream cone. 남자가 아이스크림 콘을 먹고 있다   A girl is stretching her arms out. 여자아이가 팔을 뻗고 있다   The guy is trying to stand up on the chair. 남자가 의자 위에 올라서려 하고 있다   The guy is jumping. 남자가 점프를 하고 있다   A boy is pulling a girl's hair. 남자아이가 여자아이의 머리를 잡아당기고 있다

06

A man is shaving his beard.

07

Mug has a handle.

08

Face has a mouth, a nose and eyes.

09

Airplane is one of the safest and fastest transportation.

10

50

There are fifty states in U.S.

Go on to the next step!

A man is shaving his beard. 남자가 턱수염을 깎고 있다 Mug has a handle. 머그잔은 손잡이가 있다 Face has a mouth, a nose and eyes. 얼굴에는 입, 코, 눈이 있다 Airplane is one of the safest and fastest transportation. 비행기는 가장 안전하고 빠른 운송수단 중 하나이다 There are fifty states in U.S. 미국에는 50개의 주가 있다

step 14
START ...▶

01

The guy is filling up the gas (gasoline) tank.

02

A guy is walking straight.

03

A guy whistles a song.

04

A person is washing his(her) hands with water.

05

A guy is coming down from the table.

The guy is filling up the gas (gasoline) tank. 남자가 가스(휘발유)를 채우고 있다   A guy is walking straight. 남자가 똑바로 걸어가고 있다   A guy whistles a song. 남자가 휘파람으로 노래를 부르고 있다   A person is washing his(her) hands with water. 한 사람이 물로 손을 씻고 있다   A guy is coming down from the table. 남자가 테이블에서 내려오고 있다

06

A girl has her arms crossed.

07

Supermarket sells groceries, snacks, drinks and so on.

08

80

Around the World in Eighty Days is a very popular novel around the world.

09

Umbrella is used on rainy days.

10

Frog can live both under the water and on land.

Go on to the next step!

step 15
START ···▶

01

A boy is hiding behind the box.

02

A boy is reading a book.

03

A boy is clapping his hands.

04

A boy and a girl are dancing.

05

A couple is kissing.

06

A guy is handing something over to the other guy.

07

Food is put on the plate.

08

Legs support one's weight.

09

Most of the time ladies carry a purse.

10

The early bird catches the worm.

Go on to the next step!

A guy is handing something over to the other guy. 한 남자가 다른 사람에게 뭔가를 건네 주고 있다   Food is put on the plate. 음식은 접시에 놓인다   Legs support one's weight. 다리는 사람의 무게를 지탱한다   Most of the time ladies carry a purse. 대부분의 경우 여자들은 핸드백을 가지고 다닌다   The early bird catches the worm. 일찍 일어나는 새가 벌레를 잡는다

step 16

START ···▶

01

The guy is lifting the table up.

02

A guy is sleeping on the floor.

03

A guy is reaching out his hand for a child.

04

A boy is walking inside the house.

05

A guy is picking up the cucumber from the floor.

The guy is lifting the table up. 남자가 테이블을 들어 올리고 있다   A guy is sleeping on the floor. 남자가 바닥에서 자고 있다   A guy is reaching out his hand for a child. 한 남자가 아이에게 손을 내밀고 있다   A boy is walking inside the house. 남자아이가 집 안으로 걸어 들어가고 있다   A guy is picking up the cucumber from the floor. 남자가 바닥에서 오이를 집어 올리고 있다

06

A guy is sweeping the floor with a broom.

07

Every building must have a window.

08

The glass is empty.

09

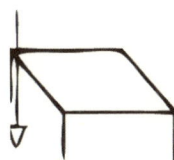

Put a chair next to the table.

10

17

Seventeen is a very popular magazine among American teenaged girls.

Go on to the next step!

A guy is sweeping the floor with a broom. 한 남자가 빗자루로 바닥을 쓸고 있다 Every building must have a window. 모든 건물에는 창문이 있어야 한다 The glass is empty. 그 잔은 비어 있다 Put a chair next to the table. 테이블 옆에 의자를 하나 놓아라
Seventeen is a very popular magazine among American teenaged girls. *세븐틴*은 미국 십대 소녀들에게 아주 인기 있는 잡지이다

step 17
START ···▶

Two guys are exchanging a high-five.

A boy is taking his hat off.

Two guys are shaking hands.

A guy is tying his dog to the table.

A guy pours trashes out on the table.

Two guys are exchanging a high-five. 두 남자가 하이파이브를 하고 있다   A boy is taking his hat off. 남자가 모자를 벗고 있다
Two guys are shaking hands. 두 남자가 악수를 하고 있다   A guy is tying his dog to the table. 남자가 개를 테이블에 묶고 있다   A guy pours trashes out on the table. 남자가 테이블 위에 쓰레기를 붓고 있다

06

A guy is squeezing the newspaper.

07

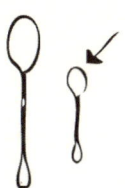

Teaspoon is used when drinking tea.

08

Orange skin is rough.

09

There are eggs in the basket.

10

Comb is used for fixing hair.

Go on to the next step!

A guy is squeezing the newspaper. 한 남자가 신문을 꽉 쥐고 있다   Teaspoon is used when drinking tea. 티스푼은 차를 마실 때 쓴다   Orange skin is rough. 오렌지 껍질은 거칠다   There are eggs in the basket. 계란이 바구니 안에 들어 있다   Comb is used for fixing hair. 빗은 머리를 정돈할 때 쓴다

step 18
START ⋯▶

01

A boy is putting his hat on.

02

A guy is walking back and forth around the chair.

03

A girl is turning around.

04

A boy inflates the balloon.

05

A guy steps into the basket.

A boy is putting his hat on. 남자아이가 모자를 쓰고 있다 A guy is walking back and forth around the chair. 한 남자가 의자 주위를 왔다 갔다 하고 있다 A girl is turning around. 여자아이가 돌고 있다 A boy inflates the balloon. 남자아이가 풍선을 분다 A guy steps into the basket. 남자가 바구니 안에 발을 들여놓는다

06

A boy is cutting a paper.

07

Strawberry is a kind of fruit.

08

40

Ali Baba and The Forty Thieves is a very famous Arabian childrens story around the world.

09

Briefcase is used for carrying papers and documents.

10

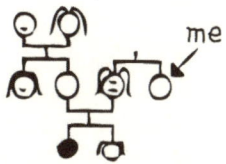

The boy is nephew to the man.

Go on to the next step!

A boy is cutting a paper. 남자아이가 종이를 자르고 있다   Strawberry is a kind of fruit. 딸기는 과일의 일종이다   Ali Baba and The Forty Thieves is a very famous Arabian childrens story around the world. 알리바바와 40인의 도적은 세계적으로 유명한 아라비아의 동화이다   Briefcase is used for carrying papers and documents. 서류 가방은 서류와 문서 따위를 운반하는 데 쓴다   The boy is nephew to the man. 그 소년은 남자의 조카(남자)이다

step 19

START ...▶

01

A guy chugs the water.

02

The guy is filling up the gas (gasoline) tank.

03

One boy is hitting the other boy on the head.

04

A guy is putting a box on the table.

05

A guy is climbing down the ladder.

A guy chugs the water. 남자가 물을 단숨에 들이킨다   The guy is filling up the gas (gasoline) tank. 남자가 가스(휘발유)를 채우고 있다   One boy is hitting the other boy on the head. 한 소년이 다른 소년의 머리를 때리고 있다   A guy is putting a box on the table. 남자가 상자를 책상 위에 놓고 있다   A guy is climbing down the ladder. 남자가 사다리를 내려오고 있다

06

A boy is wearing a hat.

07

A book is already opened up.

08

Fork is used to eat food.

09

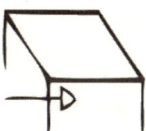

There is nothing under the table.

10

100

Go on to the next step!

A hundred years is called a century.

A boy is wearing a hat. 남자아이가 모자를 쓰고 있다   A book is already opened up. 그 책은 이미 펼쳐져 있다   Fork is used to eat food. 포크는 음식을 먹는 데 쓴다   There is nothing under the table. 테이블 밑에는 아무것도 없다   A hundred years is called a century. 일백 년은 한 세기라고도 불리운다

step 20
START ...▶

01

A guy is sweeping the floor with a broom.

02

A guy is running fast.

03

A boy inflates the balloon.

04

A guy is squeezing the newspaper.

05

A guy pours trashes out on the table.

A guy is sweeping the floor with a broom. 남자가 빗자루로 바닥을 쓸고 있다   A guy is running fast. 남자가 빠르게 달리고 있다   A boy inflates the balloon 소년이 풍선을 분다   A guy is squeezing the newspaper. 남자가 신문을 꽉 쥐고 있다   A guy pours trashes out on the table. 남자가 테이블 위에 쓰레기를 쏟는다

06

A lady opens her mouth.

07

Hat helps to block the sunlight.

08

It's a picture of a guy.

09

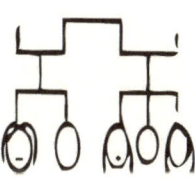

The boys and girls are cousins.

10

Go on to the next Lesson!

Orange is sweet and sour.

A lady opens her mouth. 여자가 입을 벌린다   Hat helps to block the sunlight. 모자는 햇빛을 막는 걸 도와준다   It's a picture of a guy. 그것은 한 남자의 사진이다   The boys and girls are cousins. 소년과 소녀들은 사촌지간이다   Orange is sweet and sour. 오렌지는 새콤달콤하다

Lesson 7

step 21

START ...▶

01

A boy is sticking his tongue out.

02

One guy slaps the other guy in the face.

03

A person is washing his(her) hands with water.

04

A guy is closing a small box.

05

The boy is answering the phone.

06

A guy is breathing deeply.

07

The basket is empty.

08

There is a napkin next to the fork.

09

Both male and female wear pants.

10

Ladder is used to reach the higher or lower place.

Go on to the next step!

A guy is breathing deeply. 남자가 깊게 숨을 쉬고 있다   The basket is empty. 그 바구니는 비어 있다   There is a napkin next to the fork. 포크 옆에 냅킨이 있다   Both male and female wear pants. 남성과 여성 둘 다 바지를 입는다   Ladder is used to reach the higher or lower place. 사다리는 높은 곳이나 낮은 곳에 도달하기 위해 쓴다

step 22
START ⋯▶

01

A boy is reading a book.

02

A guy is picking up the cucumber from the floor.

03

A guy is coming down from the table.

04

A guy is showing a picture.

05

A boy is combing his hair.

A boy is reading a book. 남자아이가 책을 읽고 있다   A guy is picking up the cucumber from the floor. 남자가 바닥에서 오이를 집어 올리고 있다   A guy is coming down from the table. 남자가 테이블에서 내려오고 있다   A guy is showing a picture. 한 남자가 사진을 보여 주고 있다   A boy is combing his hair. 소년이 머리를 빗고 있다

06

The guy is trying to stand up on the chair.

07

Wine is made of grapes.

08

Spider is an insect.

09

Horse was a transportation in the past.

10

14

Go on to the next step!

February 14th is Valentine's Day.

The guy is trying to stand up on the chair. 남자가 의자 위에 올라서려 하고 있다   Wine is made of grapes. 와인은 포도로 만들어진다   Spider is an insect. 거미는 곤충이다   Horse was a transportation in the past. 말은 과거에 운송 수단이었다   February 14th is Valentine's Day. 2월 14일은 밸런타인데이이다

step 23
START ...▶

01

A guy is lying down on the bed.

02

A boy is taking his hat off.

03

A boy is hiding behind the box.

04

A guy is eating an ice cream cone.

05

A boy is walking inside the house.

A guy is lying down on the bed. 남자가 침대에 눕고 있다   A boy is taking his hat off. 소년이 모자를 벗고 있다   A boy is hiding behind the box. 남자아이가 상자 뒤에 숨어 있다   A guy is eating an ice cream cone. 한 남자가 아이스크림 콘을 먹고 있다   A boy is walking inside the house. 소년이 집 안으로 걸어 들어가고 있다

06

A boy is standing upside down.

07

Cucumber is a kind of vegetable.

08

Ears are for hearing.

09

15

In basketball, each quarter is fifteen minutes.

10

Go on to the next step!

Landscape painting is a drawing of surrounding nature.

A boy is standing upside down. 남자아이가 거꾸로 서 있다   Cucumber is a kind of vegetable. 오이는 채소의 일종이다   Ears are for hearing. 귀는 듣기 위해 있다   In basketball, each quarter is fifteen minutes. 농구에서 각 쿼터는 15분이다   Landscape painting is a drawing of surrounding nature. 풍경화는 주위 자연을 그린 것이다

step 24
START ···▶

A guy is shouting out loud.

A guy is walking straight.

A guy is turning a lever away from him.

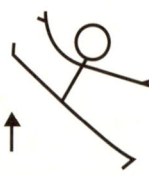

A guy raises his leg.

A guy steps into the basket.

A guy is shouting out loud. 남자가 크게 소리치고 있다   A guy is walking straight. 한 남자가 똑바로 걷고 있다   A guy is turning a lever away from him. 남자가 바깥쪽으로 레버를 돌리고 있다   A guy raises his leg. 남자가 다리를 들어 올린다   A guy steps into the basket. 한 사내가 바구니 안에 발을 들여놓는다

06

A boy is stretching his leg.

07

Time is valuable.

08

Thumb and little finger are the smallest fingers among five fingers.

09

A lady is wearing earrings.

10

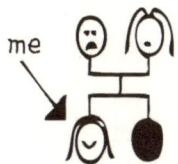

The boy is brother to the girl.

Go on to the next step!

A boy is stretching his leg. 남자아이가 다리를 스트레칭하고 있다   Time is valuable. 시간은 소중하다   Thumb and little finger are the smallest fingers among five fingers. 엄지와 새끼손가락이 다섯 손가락 중 가장 작다   A lady is wearing earrings. 여자가 귀고리를 하고 있다   The boy is brother to the girl. 그 소년은 여자아이의 남자 형제이다

step 25
START ···▶

01

A boy inflates the balloon.

02

A girl has her arms crossed.

03

A lady opens her mouth.

04

A boy is combing his hair.

05

A boy is taking his hat off.

A boy inflates the balloon. 남자아이가 풍선을 분다 A girl has her arms crossed. 여자아이가 팔을 교차시켰다 A lady opens her mouth. 여자가 입을 벌린다 A boy is combing his hair. 소년이 머리를 빗고 있다 A boy is taking his hat off. 소년이 모자를 벗고 있다

06

A guy is wiping the window with a cloth.

07

Pineapple is a tropical fruit.

08

Thumb and ring finger are tied to strings.

09

Every household, in these days, has at least one television.

10

50

There are 50 states in U.S.

Go on to the next step!

step 26

START ···▶

A guy steps into the basket.

A guy is lighting up the candles.

The boy is answering the phone.

A guy is smelling the cucumber.

The guy is stuck under the table.

A guy steps into the basket. 한 남자가 바구니 안에 발을 들여놓는다   A guy is lighting up the candles. 남자가 촛불을 켜고 있다
The boy is answering the phone. 남자아이가 전화를 받고 있다   A guy is smelling the cucumber. 한 사내가 오이 냄새를 맡고 있다
The guy is stuck under the table. 남자가 테이블 밑에 갇혀 있다

06

A boy is hiding behind the box.

07

The light bulb is on.

08

Library loans out the books to people.

09

This is a button down shirt.

10

Scissors are for cutting things.

Go on to the next step!

A boy is hiding behind the box. 남자아이가 상자 뒤에 숨어 있다   The light bulb is on. 전구가 켜져 있다   Library loans out the books to people. 도서관은 사람들에게 책을 빌려 준다   This is a button down shirt. 이것은 단추가 달린 셔츠이다   Scissors are for cutting things. 가위는 물건을 자르는 데 쓴다

01

step 27
START ...▶

A guy is putting a box on the table.

02

A boy is counting with the fingers.

03

A guy whistles a song.

04

A guy is picking up the cucumber from the floor.

05

A guy is climbing down the ladder.

A guy is putting a box on the table. 한 남자가 테이블 위에 상자를 놓고 있다   A boy is counting with the fingers. 남자아이가 손가락으로 수를 세고 있다   A guy whistles a song. 남자가 휘파람으로 노래를 부른다   A guy is picking up the cucumber from the floor. 남자가 바닥에서 오이를 집어 올리고 있다   A guy is climbing down the ladder. 남자가 사다리에서 내려오고 있다

06

A guy is shouting out loud.

07

Ice cream cone is sweet.

08

Show me your back.

09

The candle is lit up.

10

18

Go on to the next step!

In America, when a person is eighteen, he or she is treated as an adult.

A guy is shouting out loud. 남자가 크게 소리치고 있다   Ice cream cone is sweet. 아이스크림 콘은 달다   Show me your back. 내게 등을 보여 줘   The candle is lit up. 초에 불이 켜졌다   In America, when a person is eighteen, he or she is treated as an adult. 미국에선 18살이면 성인 대우를 받는다

step 28
START ...▶

A couple is kissing.

02

A guy is going up the stairs.

03

A guy is sweeping the floor with a broom.

04

The guy turns on the light bulb.

05

A guy is showing a picture.

A couple is kissing. 커플이 키스를 하고 있다   A guy is going up the stairs. 남자가 계단을 오르고 있다   A guy is sweeping the floor with a broom. 남자가 빗자루로 바닥을 쓸고 있다   The guy turns on the light bulb. 남자가 전구를 켠다   A guy is showing a picture. 한 남자가 사진을 보여 주고 있다

06

The lady winks with her left eye.

07

Pencil is one of the writing instruments.

08

Scissors are for cutting things.

09

The house has 4 walls.

10

People who have bad eyesight wear glasses.

Go on to the next step!

The lady winks with her left eye. 여자가 왼쪽 눈으로 윙크한다 Pencil is one of the writing instruments 연필은 필기구 중 하나이다 Scissors are for cutting things. 가위는 물건들을 자르는 데 쓰인다 The house has 4 walls. 그 집은 사면이 벽이다 People who have bad eyesight wear glasses. 시력이 나쁜 사람들은 안경을 쓴다

step 29
START ···▶

01

A boy is putting his hat on.

02

A boy is going to school.

03

The guy is filling up the gas (gasoline) tank.

04

A guy is tying his dog to the table.

05

A boy is wearing a hat.

A boy is putting his hat on. 남자아이가 모자를 쓰고 있다   A boy is going to school. 소년이 학교에 가고 있다   The guy is filling up the gas (gasoline) tank. 남자가 가스(휘발유)를 채우고 있다   A guy is tying his dog to the table. 한 사내가 개를 테이블에 묶고 있다   A boy is wearing a hat. 소년이 모자를 쓰고 있다

06

A boy is sticking his tongue out.

07

There is a box standing against the wall.

08

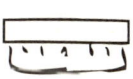

The eraser is for a blackboard.

09

The girl is daughter to the man.

10

The lamp is sitting on the table.

Go on to the next step!

A boy is sticking his tongue out. 남자아이가 혀를 내밀고 있다 There is a box standing against the wall. 상자가 벽에 맞대어 있다 The eraser is for a blackboard. 그 지우개는 칠판용이다 The girl is daughter to the man. 여자아이는 그 남자의 딸이다 The lamp is sitting on the table. 램프가 테이블 위에 있다

step 30
START ···▶

01

One guy slaps the other guy in the face.

02

The guy is pushing the table.

03

A guy raises his hand.

04

A guy is handing something over to the other guy.

05

A guy is lying down on the bed.

One guy slaps the other guy in the face. 한 남자가 다른 남자의 얼굴을 때린다   The guy is pushing the table. 남자가 테이블을 밀고 있다   A guy raises his hand. 한 사내가 팔을 든다   A guy is handing something over to the other guy. 한 남자가 다른 남자에게 무언가를 건네고 있다   A guy is lying down on the bed. 남자가 침대에 눕고 있다

06

A guy is holding the other guy by the arms.

07

Pear is a kind of fruit.

08

100

A hundred years is called a century.

09

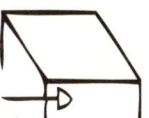

There is nothing under the table.

10

A guy is sweeping the floor with a broom.

● ● ● ▶

Go on to the next Lesson!

A guy is holding the other guy by the arms. 한 남자가 다른 남자의 팔을 잡고 있다   Pear is a kind of fruit. 배는 과일의 일종이다   A hundred years is called a century. 일백 년은 한 세기라고 불린다   There is nothing under the table. 테이블 밑에 아무것도 없다   A guy is sweeping the floor with a broom. 한 남자가 빗자루로 바닥을 쓸고 있다

Lesson 8

step 31
START ⋯▶

01

A guy whistles a song.

02

A guy is holding the other guy by the arms.

03

A boy is reading a book.

04

The guy is trying to stand up on the chair.

05

A guy is turning a lever away from him.

A guy whistles a song. 한 남자가 휘파람으로 노래를 부르고 있다 A guy is holding the other guy by the arms. 한 남자가 다른 남자의 팔을 잡고 있다 A boy is reading a book. 남자아이가 책을 읽고 있다 The guy is trying to stand up on the chair. 남자가 의자에 올라서려 하고 있다 A guy is turning a lever away from him. 한 남자가 바깥쪽으로 레버를 돌리고 있다

오디오 QR 코드
Lesson 8

06

A guy is squeezing the newspaper.

07

The door is closed.

08

Show me your back.

09

A chair and desk are combined together.

10

40

Go on to the next step!

Ali Baba and The forty Thieves is a very famous Arabian childrens story around the world.

A guy is squeezing the newspaper. 한 사내가 신문을 꽉 쥐고 있다 The door is closed. 문이 닫혀 있다 Show me your back. 내게 등을 보여 줘 A chair and desk are combined together. 의자와 책상이 함께 붙어 있다 *Ali Baba and The forty Thieves* is a very famous Arabian childrens story around the world. *알리바바와 40인의 도적*은 세계적으로 유명한 아라비안 동화이다

step 32
START ...▶

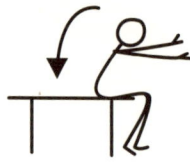

A guy is sitting on the table.

A boy is wearing a hat.

A boy and a girl are dancing.

A guy steps into the basket.

A guy is sweeping the floor with a broom.

A guy is sitting on the table. 한 남자가 테이블 위에 앉고 있다   A boy is wearing a hat. 소년이 모자를 쓰고 있다   A boy and a girl are dancing. 소년과 소녀가 춤을 추고 있다   A guy steps into the basket. 한 남자가 바구니에 발을 들여놓는다   A guy is sweeping the floor with a broom. 사내가 빗자루로 바닥을 쓸고 있다

06

The guy is filling up the gas (gasoline) tank.

07

Christians go to church on Sundays.

08

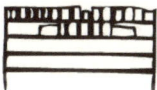

Books are organized on the bookshelf.

09

The early bird catches the worm.

10

Scissors are for cutting things.

Go on to the next step!

step 33

START ···▶

01

A guy is shouting out loud.

02

A guy is putting a box on the table.

03

A boy is sticking his tongue out.

04

The guy is stuck under the table.

05

A guy is tying his dog to the table.

A guy is shouting out loud. 한 남자가 크게 소리 지르고 있다   A guy is putting a box on the table. 남자가 테이블 위에 상자를 놓고 있다   A boy is sticking his tongue out. 소년이 혀를 내밀고 있다   The guy is stuck under the table. 한 남자가 책상 밑에 갇혀 있다   A guy is tying his dog to the table. 한 남자가 개를 테이블에 묶고 있다

06

The boy is answering the phone.

07

A saucer is used for supporting a cup.

08

Everyone looks forward to Saturdays.

09

Keep the trash can outside the house.

10

Go on to the next step!

Flashlight is portable.

The boy is answering the phone. 소년이 전화를 받고 있다   A saucer is used for supporting a cup. 받침 접시는 컵을 받치는 데 쓴다
Everyone looks forward to Saturdays. 모든 사람들이 토요일을 기대한다   Keep the trash can outside the house. 쓰레기통은 집 밖에 두어라   Flashlight is portable. 손전등은 휴대용이다

step 34

START ···▶

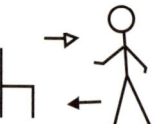

A guy is walking back and forth around the chair.

02

The guy is pushing the table.

03

A boy is stretching his leg.

04

A boy is clapping.

05

One guy slaps the other guy in the face.

06

A boy is pulling a girl's hair.

07

Dog is one of the most popular pet.

08

90

Right angle is ninety degrees.

09

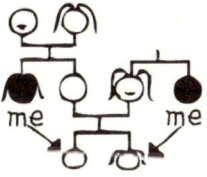

The woman and man are aunt and uncle to the boy and girl.

10

A lady is wearing earrings.

••• ▶

Go on to the next step!

A boy is pulling a girl's hair. 소년이 소녀의 머리를 잡아당기고 있다   Dog is one of the most popular pet. 개는 가장 인기 있는 애완동물 중 하나이다   Right angle is ninety degrees. 직각은 90도이다   The woman and man are aunt and uncle to the boy and girl. 그 여자와 남자는 소년과 소녀의 고모와 삼촌이다   A lady is wearing earrings. 여자가 귀고리를 하고 있다

step 35
START ...▶

01

A guy is lifting a small chair.

02

The guy is stopping something (someone).

03

A beggar is begging for money.

04

A guy turns the light bulb off.

05

A boy is combing his hair.

A guy is lifting a small chair. 남자가 작은 의자를 들어 올리고 있다   The guy is stopping something (someone). 남자가 무언가(누군가)를 멈춰 세우고 있다   A beggar is begging for money. 거지가 돈을 구걸하고 있다   A guy turns the light bulb off. 남자가 전등를 끈다   A boy is combing his hair. 소년이 머리를 빗고 있다

06

A girl is turning the lever toward her.

07

Bottle is recyclable.

08

Face has a mouth, a nose, and eyes.

09

People who have bad eyesight wear glasses.

10

60

Go on to the next step!

There are sixty minutes in an hour, and sixty seconds in a minute.

A girl is turning the lever toward her. 소녀가 안쪽으로 레버를 돌리고 있다   Bottle is recyclable. 유리병은 재활용할 수 있다   Face has a mouth, a nose, and eyes. 얼굴에는 입, 코, 눈이 있다   People who have bad eyesight wear glasses. 시력이 나쁜 사람들은 안경을 쓴다   There are sixty minutes in an hour, and sixty seconds in a minute. 한 시간은 60분, 1분은 60초이다

step 36
START ...▶

01

The guy is picking up a cucumber from the floor.

02

One boy is hitting the other boy on the head.

03

A boy is walking out of the house.

04

A guy is holding his arms up.

05

A guy is showing a picture.

The guy is picking up a cucumber from the floor. 남자가 바닥에서 오이를 집어 올리고 있다   One boy is hitting the other boy on the head. 한 소년이 다른 소년의 머리를 때리고 있다   A boy is walking out of the house. 소년이 집 밖으로 걸어 나오고 있다   A guy is holding his arms up. 남자가 두 팔을 들고 있다   A guy is showing a picture. 남자가 사진을 보여 주고 있다

06

A boy is pouring the water into a glass.

07

Pepper is used as a spice for many kinds of food.

08

Rabbit is very fast.

09

11

In soccer, eleven players from each team play on the field.

10

Go on to the next step!

Key opens locks and doors.

A boy is pouring the water into a glass. 남자아이가 잔에 물을 따르고 있다 Pepper is used as a spice for many kinds of food. 고추는 많은 음식에 양념으로 쓰인다 Rabbit is very fast. 토끼는 매우 빠르다 In soccer, eleven players from each team play on the field. 축구에선 각 팀별로 11명의 선수들이 경기장에서 경기를 한다 Key opens locks and doors. 열쇠는 자물쇠와 문을 연다

step 37

START ···▶

A guy is putting a cucumber into the box.

A boy is pouring the water into a glass.

One boy is hitting the other boy on the head.

A guy is putting a box on the table.

A couple is kissing.

A guy is putting a cucumber into the box. 남자가 오이를 상자 안에 넣고 있다   A boy is pouring the water into a glass. 소년이 잔에 물을 따르고 있다   One boy is hitting the other boy on the head. 한 소년이 다른 소년의 머리를 때리고 있다   A guy is putting a box on the table. 남자가 테이블에 상자를 놓고 있다   A couple is kissing. 커플이 키스를 하고 있다

06

A guy is squeezing the newspaper.

07

Girls wear dresses.

08

15

In basketball, each quarter is fifteen minutes.

09

Wedding ring is worn on the fourth finger of the left hand.

10

Squirrel is very small and quick.

Go on to the next step!

A guy is squeezing the newspaper. 남자가 신문을 꽉 쥐고 있다   Girls wear dresses. 소녀들은 드레스를 입는다   In basketball, each quarter is fifteen minutes. 농구에서 각 쿼터는 15분이다   Wedding ring is worn on the fourth finger of the left hand. 결혼반지는 왼손 넷째 손가락에 낀다   Squirrel is very small and quick. 다람쥐는 매우 작고 잽싸다

step 38
START ···▶

01

A boy is picking his ear.

02

A guy is turning a lever away from him.

03

A boy is reading a book.

04

A boy inflates the balloon.

05

A man is shaving his beard.

A boy is picking his ear. 소년이 귀를 후비고 있다   A guy is turning a lever away from him. 남자가 바깥쪽으로 레버를 돌리고 있다   A boy is reading a book. 소년이 책을 읽고 있다   A boy inflates the balloon. 소년이 풍선을 분다   A man is shaving his beard. 남자가 면도를 하고 있다

06

A guy is climbing down the ladder.

07

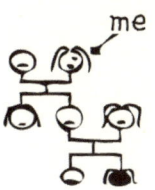

The girl is granddaughter to the woman.

08

Wine is made of grapes.

09

19

The nineteenth century saw the industrial revolution.

10

Go on to the next step!

There are a telephone, radio and a photo on the desk.

A guy is climbing down the ladder. 남자가 계단에서 내려오고 있다   The girl is granddaughter to the woman. 그 소녀는 여자의 손녀이다   Wine is made of grapes. 와인은 포도로 만들어진다   The nineteenth century saw the industrial revolution. 19세기에 산업혁명이 발생했다   There are a telephone, radio and a photo on the desk. 책상 위에 전화, 라디오, 사진이 있다

Lesson 8 **171**

step 39
START ···▶

A boy is stretching his leg.

01

02

A guy is lifting a girl over his head.

03

The guy is filling up the gas (gasoline) tank.

04

A guy is lighting up the candles.

05

A guy is reaching out his hand for a child.

A boy is stretching his leg. 소년이 다리를 스트레칭하고 있다   A guy is lifting a girl over his head. 남자가 여자아이를 머리 위로 들어 올리고 있다   The guy is filling up the gas (gasoline) tank. 남자가 가스(휘발유)를 채우고 있다   A guy is lighting up the candles. 남자가 촛불을 켜고 있다   A guy is reaching out his hand for a child. 남자가 아이에게 손을 내밀고 있다

06

A guy is sleeping on the floor.

07

We can see ourselves on a mirror because mirror reflects the light.

08

Car is the most common transportation in the world.

09

Horse was a transportation in the past.

10

50

There are fifty states in U.S.

Go on to the next step!

step 40
START ···▶

01

A guy is wiping the window with a cloth.

02

A guy pours trash out on the table.

03

A girl is turning the lever toward her.

04

A guy is raising his leg.

05

A guy is going up the stairs.

A guy is wiping the window with a cloth. 남자가 걸레로 창문을 닦고 있다   A guy pours trash out on the table. 한 남자가 책상 위에 쓰레기를 쏟는다   A girl is turning the lever toward her. 여자아이가 안쪽으로 레버를 돌리고 있다   A guy is raising his leg. 남자가 다리를 올리고 있다   A guy is going up the stairs. 한 남자가 계단을 오르고 있다

06

A girl is opening her mouth.

07

Movie house shows the movies.

08

There are twelve months in a year.

09

There are eggs in the basket.

10

The lamp is sitting on the table.

Go on to the next step!

A girl is opening her mouth. 여자아이가 입을 벌리고 있다   Movie house shows the movies. 영화관에선 영화를 보여 준다   There are twelve months in a year. 일년은 열두 달이다   There are eggs in the basket. 바구니에 계란들이 있다   The lamp is sitting on the table. 램프가 테이블 위에 있다

step 41

START ···▶

01

One guy slaps the other guy in the face.

02

The guy is stuck under the table.

03

A guy is climbing down the ladder.

04

A guy chugs the water.

05

Two guys are exchanging a high-five.

One guy slaps the other guy in the face. 한 남자가 다른 남자의 얼굴을 때린다   The guy is stuck under the table. 한 사내가 테이블 밑에 갇혀 있다   A guy is climbing down the ladder. 사내가 사다리를 내려오고 있다   A guy chugs the water. 한 사내가 물을 단숨에 들이킨다   Two guys are exchanging a high-five. 두 사람이 하이파이브를 하고 있다

06

A guy is lying down on the bed.

07

70

Seventy percent of the human body is composed of water.

08

Umbrella is used on rainy days.

09

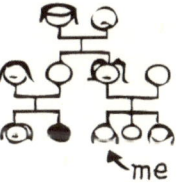

The boy and the girl are cousins.

10

•••▶

Go on to the next step!

Ladder is used to reach the higher or lower place.

A guy is lying down on the bed. 한 남자가 침대에 눕고 있다   Seventy percent of the human body is composed of water. 사람 몸의 70%는 수분으로 구성되어 있다   Umbrella is used on rainy days. 우산은 비 오는 날에 쓴다   The boy and the girl are cousins. 소년과 소녀는 사촌지간이다   Ladder is used to reach the higher or lower place. 사다리는 높은 곳이나 낮은 곳에 이르기 위해 사용된다

step 42
START ···▶

01

A guy is handing something over to the other guy.

02

A guy is eating an ice cream cone.

03

A boy is clapping.

04

A girl is stretching her arms out.

05

A person is washing his (her) hands with the water.

A guy is handing something over to the other guy. 한 남자가 다른 남자에게 무언가를 전달하고 있다   A guy is eating an ice cream cone. 한 남자가 아이스크림 콘을 먹고 있다   A boy is clapping. 소년이 박수를 치고 있다   A girl is stretching her arms out. 소녀가 팔을 뻗고 있다   A person is washing his (her) hands with the water. 한 사람이 물로 손을 씻고 있다

06

A girl is dancing.

07

Women's restroom is only for females.

08

Fish lives under the water.

09

A chair and a desk are combined together.

10

11

Go on to the next Chapter!

In soccer, eleven players from each team play on the field.

A girl is dancing. 소녀가 춤추고 있다   Women's restroom is only for females. 여자 화장실은 여성 전용이다   Fish lives under the water. 물고기는 물에서 산다   A chair and a desk are combined together. 의자와 책상이 붙어 있다   In soccer, eleven players from each team play on the field. 축구는 각 팀별로 11명의 선수가 경기장에서 경기를 한다

ENGLISH
ICEBREAK

CHAPTER 3

Lesson 1 -4   Dictation Sheets 1

Lesson 1

step 01
START ...▶

<u>01</u>

<u>02</u>

<u>03</u>

<u>04</u>

<u>05</u>

06

07

08

09

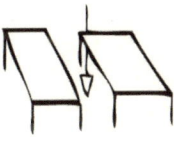

10

•••▶

Go on to the next step!

step 02
START ...▶

01

02

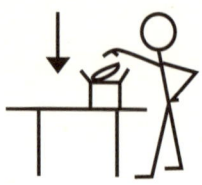

03

04

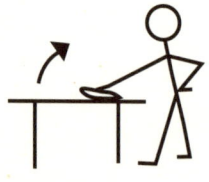

05

06

07

08

09

10

Go on to the next step!

step 03
START ⋯▶

<u>01</u>

....
....

<u>02</u>

....
....

<u>03</u>

....
....

<u>04</u>

....
....

<u>05</u>

....
....

06

07

08

09

10

Go on to the next step!

step 04
START ···▶

01

02

03

04

05

06

07

....
....

....
....

08

09

....
....

....
....

10

•••▶

Go on to the next step!

....
....

Lesson 1

step 05
START ...▶

01

02

03

04
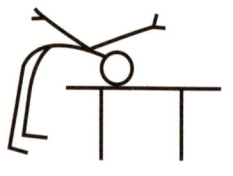

05

06

07

08

09

10

Go on to the next step!

step 06
START ...▶

01

02

03

04

05

06

07

08
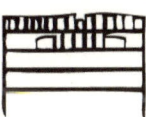

09

10

 Go on to the next step!

step 07
START ...▶

01

02

03

04

05

06

07

08

09

10

Go on to the next step!

step 08
START ...▶

01

02
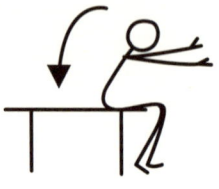

03

04

05

06

07

08

09

10

Go on to the next step!

step 09
START ···▶

01

02

03

04

05
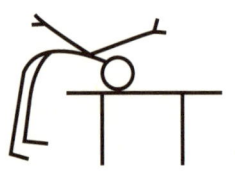

06

07

08

09

10

7

•••▶

Go on to the next step!

step 10
START ...▶

01

02

03

04

05

06

....
....

07

....
....

08

....
....

09

....
....

10

....
....

●●● ▶

Go on to the next Lesson!

Lesson 1

Lesson 2

step 11
START ...▶

01

....
....

02

....
....

03

....
....

04

....
....

05

....
....

06

....
....

07

....
....

08

....
....

09

....
....

10

10

Go on to the next step!

....
....

step 12

START ···▶

01

02

03

04

05

06

....
....

07

....
....

08

....
....

09

....
....

10

....
....

•••▶

Go on to the next step!

step 13
START ...▶

01

02

03

04

05

06

....
....

07

....
....

08

....
....

09

....
....

10

....
....

Go on to the next step!

step 14
START ···▶

01

02

03

04

05

06

07

08

09

10

Go on to the next step!

Lesson 2

step 15
START ···▶

01

02

03

04

05

step 16
START ···▶

01

02

03

04
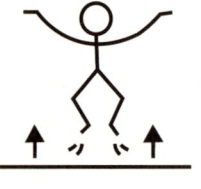

05

06

07

08

09

10

step 17
START ...▶

01

....
....

02

....
....

03

....
....

04

....
....

05

....
....

06

07

08

09

10

4

••• ▶

Go on to the next step!

step 18
START ...▶

01

02

03

04

05

06

07

08

09

10

Go on to the next step!

step 19
START ···▶

01

02

03

04

05

06

![house with $ sign]

....
....

07

![basket]

....
....

08

![face with arrows pointing to ears]

....
....

09

![cat face]

....
....

10

2

....
....

Go on to the next step!

step 20
START ...▶

01

02

03

04

05

06

07

08

09

10

Go on to the next Lesson!

Lesson 3

step 21
START ...▶

01

02

03

04

05

06

07
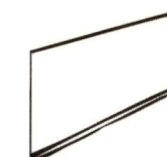

08

09

10

Go on to the next step!

step 22
START ···▶

01

02

03

04

05

06

07

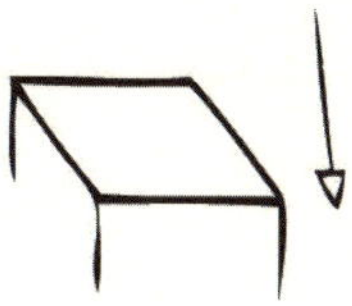

08

09

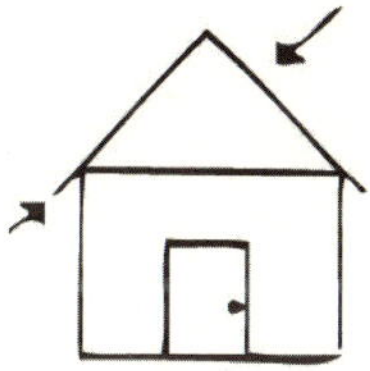

10

Go on to the next step!

Lesson 3

step 23
START ••▶

01

02

03

04

05

06

....
....

07

....
....

08

....
....

09

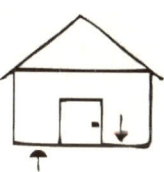

....
....

10

....
....

●●● ▶

Go on to the next step!

step 24
START ...▶

01

02

03

04

05

06

....

....

07

....

....

08

....

....

09

....

....

10

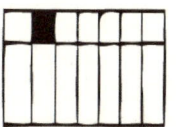

•••▶

Go on to the next step!

....

....

step 25
START ···▶

<u>01</u>

<u>02</u>

<u>03</u>

<u>04</u>

<u>05</u>

06

07

08

09

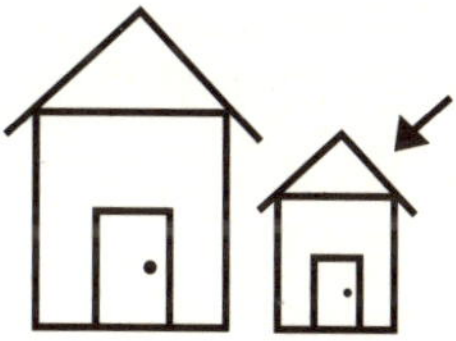

10

Go on to the next step!

Lesson 3

step 26
START ···▶

01

02

03

04

05

06

07

08

09

10

Go on to the next step!

step 27
START ···▶

01

02

03

04

05

06

07

08

09

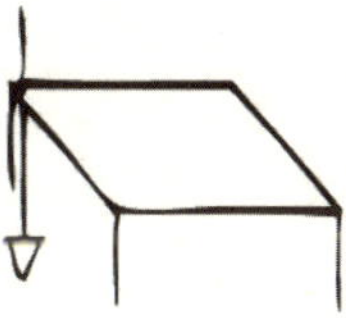

10

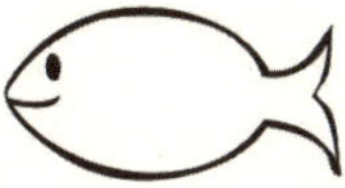

Go on to the next step!

Lesson 3

step 28
START ...▶

01

02

03

04

05

06

07

08

09

10

Go on to the next step!

step 29
START ...▶

01

02

03

04

05
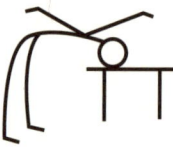

06

07

....
....

....
....

08

09

....
....

....
....

10

....
....

Go on to the next step!

step 30
START ...▶

01

02

03

04

05
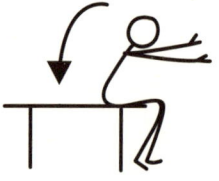

06

....
....

07

....
....

08

....
....

09

....
....

10

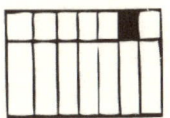

....
....

●●● ▶

Go on to the next Lesson!

Lesson 4

step 31
START ...▶

01

02

03

04

05

06

07

08

09

10

Go on to the next step!

Lesson 4

step 32
START ···▶

01

02

03

04

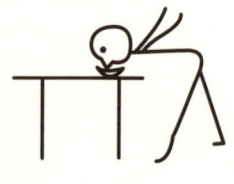

05

06

07

08
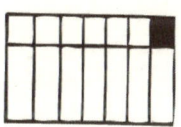

09

10
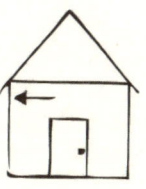

▶ Go on to the next step!

step 33
START ···▶

01

....
....

02

....
....

03

....
....

04

....
....

05

....
....

06

_____
_____

07

_____
_____

08

_____
_____

09

_____
_____

10

_____
_____

••▶

Go on to the next step!

step 34
START ...▶

01

02

03

04

05

06

....
....

07

....
....

08

....
....

09

....
....

10

....
....

Go on to the next step!

step 35

START ...▶

01

02

03

04

05

06

....
....

07

....
....

08

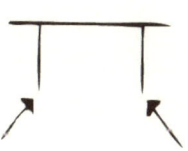

....
....

09

....
....

10

9

Go on to the next step!

....
....

step 36
START ...▶

01
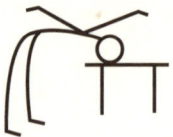

02

03

04

05

06

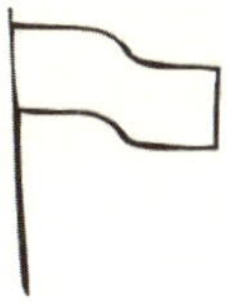

....
....

07

....
....

08

me   me

....
....

09

5

....
....

10

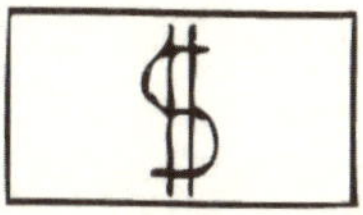

$

....
....

•••▶

Go on to the next step!

Lesson 4

step 37
START ···▶

02

03

04

05

06

....
....

07

....
....

08

....
....

09

....
....

10

....
....

Go on to the next step!

step 38
START ···▶

01

02

03

04

05

<u>06</u>

20

....
....

<u>07</u>

....
....

<u>08</u>

....
....

<u>09</u>

....
....

<u>10</u>

....
....

• • • ▶

Go on to the next step!

step 39
START ...▶

01

....
....

02

....
....

03

....
....

04

....
....

05

....
....

06

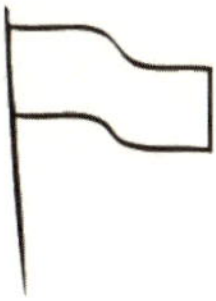

07

08

09

10

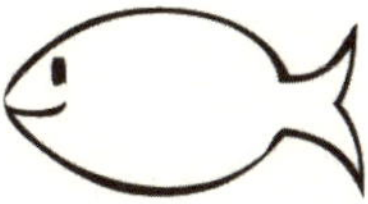

Go on to the next step!

Lesson 4

step 40
START ...▶

01

02

03

04

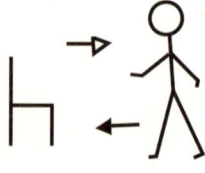

05

06

07

08

09

10

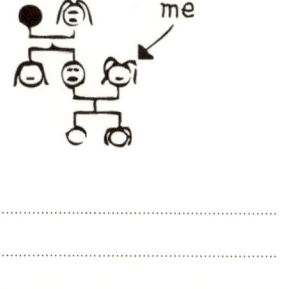

Go on to the next step!

step 41
START ⋯▶

01

02

03

04

05

06

07

08

09

10

Go on to the next step!

step 42
START ...▶

01

....
....

02

....
....

03

....
....

04

....
....

05

....
....

06

....
....

07

10

....
....

08

....
....

09

....
....

10

....
....

● ● ● ▶

Go on to the next chapter!

ENGLISH
ICEBREAK

CHAPTER 4

Lesson 5-8   Dictation Sheets 2

Lesson 5

step 01
START ...▶

01

....
....

02

....
....

03

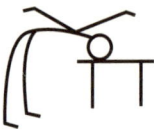

....
....

04

....
....

05

....
....

06

....
....

07

....
....

08

....
....

09

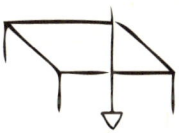

....
....

10

18

Go on to the next step!

....
....

step 02
START ···▶

01

02

03

04

05

06

....
....

07

....
....

08

....
....

09

....
....

10

14

Go on to the next step!

....
....

step 03
START ···▶

<u>01</u>

<u>02</u>

<u>03</u>

<u>04</u>

<u>05</u>

06

07

08

09

10

Go on to the next step!

step 04
START ...▶

01

....
....

02

....
....

03

....
....

04

....
....

05

....
....

06

....
....

07

....
....

08

....
....

09

20

....
....

10

....
....

•••▶

Go on to the next step!

Lesson 5

step 05
START ···▶

<u>01</u>

<u>02</u>

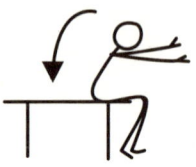

<u>03</u>

<u>04</u>

<u>05</u>

06

....
....

07

....
....

08

....
....

09

....
....

10

....
....

Go on to the next step!

step 06
START ···▶

01

02

03

04

05

06

....
....

07

....
....

08

me

....
....

09

....
....

10

....
....

● ● ● ▶

Go on to the next step!

step 07
START ...▶

01

02

03

04

05

06

....

07

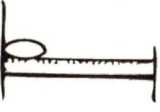

....

08

....

09

10

....

10

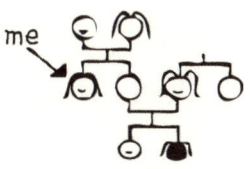

....

••• ▶

Go on to the next step!

step 08
START ...▶

01

02

03

04

05

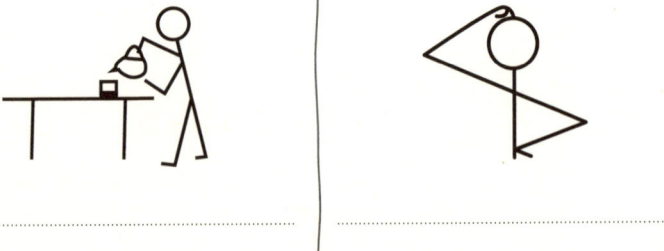

06

....
....

07

....
....

08

....
....

09

....
....

10

20

Go on to the next step!

....
....

step 09
START ...▶

01

02

03

04

05

06

....
....

07

....
....

08

....
....

09

....
....

10

....
....

• • • ▶

Go on to the next step!

step 10
START ···▶

<u>01</u>

<u>02</u>

<u>03</u>

<u>04</u>

<u>05</u>

06

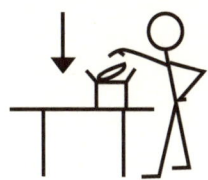

07

08

09

5

10

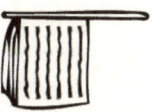

• • • ▶

Go on to the next Lesson!

Lesson 6

step 11
START ···▶

01

02

03

04

05

06

07

08

09

10

• • • ▶

Go on to the next step!

step 12
START ...▶

01

02

03

04

05

06

07

08

09

10

17

Go on to the next step!

step 13
START ···▶

01

02

03

04
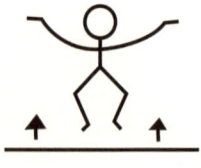

05

06

....

....

07

....

....

08

....

....

09

....

....

10

50

....

....

Go on to the next step!

step 14
START ...▶

01

02

03

04

05

06

....
....

07

....
....

08

80

....
....

09

....
....

10

....
....

●●●▶

Go on to the next step!

step 15
START ...▶

01

02

03

04

05

06

07

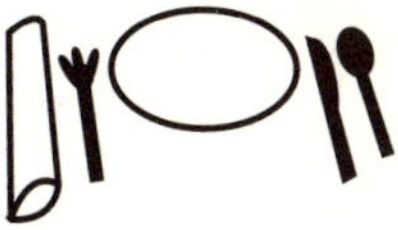

08

09

10

Go on to the next step!

Lesson 6

step 16
START ···▶

01

02

03

04

05

06

....
....

07

....
....

08

....
....

09

....
....

10

17

....
....

Go on to the next step!

step 17
START ···▶

01

....
....

02

....
....

03

....
....

04

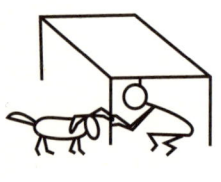

....
....

05

....
....

06

....
....

07

....
....

08

....
....

09

....
....

10

•••▶

Go on to the next step!

....
....

step 18
START ···▶

01

02
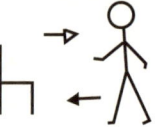

03

04

05

06

07

08

40

09

10

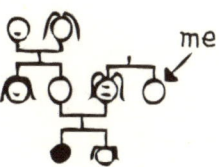

●●● ▶

Go on to the next step!

step 19
START ...▶

01

02

03

04

05

06

....
....

07

....
....

08

....
....

09

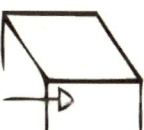

....
....

10

100

Go on to the next step!

....
....

step 20
START ···▶

01

02

03

04

05

06

....
....

07

....
....

08

....
....

09
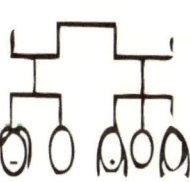

....
....

10

....
....

•••▶

Go on to the next Lesson!

Lesson 7

step 21
START ...▶

01

02

03

04

05

06

07

08

09

10

Go on to the next step!

step 22
START ···▶

01

02

03

04

05

06

....
....

07

....
....

08

....
....

09

....
....

10

14

Go on to the next step!

....
....

step 23
START ...▶

01

....
....

02

....
....

03

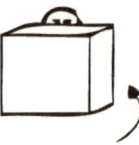

....
....

04

....
....

05

....
....

06

07

08

09

15

10

•••▶

Go on to the next step!

step 24

START ...▶

01

02

03

04

05

06

....
....

07

....
....

08

....
....

09

....
....

10

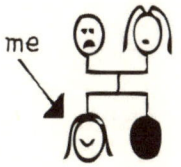

....
....

● ● ● ▶

Go on to the next step!

step 25
START ...▶

01

02

03

04

05

06

....
....

07

....
....

08

....
....

09

....
....

10

50

....
....

Go on to the next step!

step 26
START ···▶

01

02

03

04

05

06

07

08

09

10

Go on to the next step!

step 27
START ...▶

01

02

03

04

05

06

....
....

07

....
....

08

....
....

09

....
....

10

18

....
....

Go on to the next step!

step 28
START ...▶

01

02

03

04

05

06

07

08

09

10

Go on to the next step!

step 29
START ...▶

01

02

03

04

05

06

07

08

09

10

Go on to the next step!

step 30
START ···▶

01

02

03

04

05

06

....
....

07

....
....

08

100

....
....

09

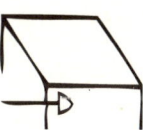

....
....

10

....
....

Go on to the next Lesson!

Lesson 8

step 31
START ···▶

01

....
....

02

....
....

03

....
....

04

....
....

05

....
....

06

....
....

07

....
....

08

....
....

09

....
....

10

40

....
....

Go on to the next step!

step 32
START ...▶

01
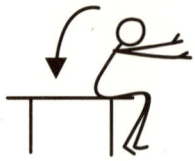

02

03

04

05

06

_____
_____

07

_____
_____

08

_____
_____

09

_____
_____

10

_____
_____

••• ▶

Go on to the next step!

step 33
START ...▶

01

....
....

02

....
....

03

....
....

04

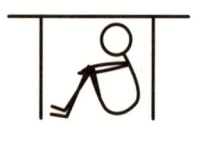

....
....

05

....
....

06

07

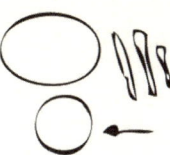

08

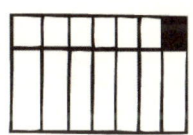

09

10

• • • ▶

Go on to the next step!

step 34
START ···▶

01

02

03

04

05

06

07

08
90

09
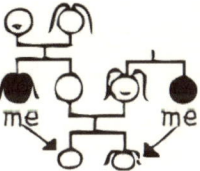

10

••• ▶
Go on to the next step!

step 35
START ···▶

01

....
....

02

....
....

03

....
....

04

....
....

05

....
....

06

....
....

07

....
....

08
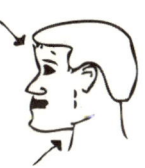

....
....

09

....
....

10

60

Go on to the next step!

....
....

step 36
START ···▶

01

02

03

04

05

06

_____
_____

07

_____
_____

08

_____
_____

09

11

_____
_____

10

_____
_____

•••▶

Go on to the next step!

step 37
START ···▶

01

02

03

04

05

06

07

08

15

09

10

•••▶

Go on to the next step!

step 38
START ···▶

01

02

03

04

05

06

....
....

07

....
....

08

....
....

09

19

....
....

10

....
....

•••▶

Go on to the next step!

step 39
START ···▶

01

....
....

02

....
....

03

....
....

04

....
....

05

....
....

06

07

....
....

....
....

08

09

....
....

....
....

10

50

Go on to the next step!

....
....

step 40
START ···▶

01

02

03

04

05

06

....
....

07

....
....

08

12

....
....

09

....
....

10

....
....

•••▶

Go on to the next step!

step 41
START ···▶

<u>01</u>

<u>02</u>

<u>03</u>

<u>04</u>

<u>05</u>

06

....
....

07

70

....
....

08

....
....

09

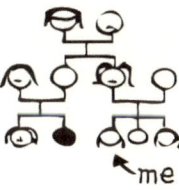

....
....

10

....
....

● ● ● ▶

Go on to the next step!

step 42
START ...▶

01

02

03

04

05

06

07

08

09

10

11   ...▶ END

ENGLISH
ICEBREAK